Twenty-Six Years' Reminiscences of Scotch Grouse Moors

The Strath of Dalnawillan,
FROM THE MOUND POOL.

AFTER A PICTURE BY DOUGLAS ADAMS.

TWENTY-SIX YEARS

Reminiscences

OF

Scotch Grouse Moors.

———⚬o⟡⚬⟡o⚬———

By W. A. ADAMS.

———⚬o⟡⚬⟡o⚬———

THE ILLUSTRATIONS DRAWN BY C. WHYMPER.

LONDON:

HORACE COX,

"THE FIELD" OFFICE, 346, STRAND, W.C.

——

1889.

LONDON:

PRINTED BY HORACE COX, 346, STRAND, W.C.

CONTENTS.

"The first gleam of light on Pickering Moor."

TWENTY-SIX YEARS REMINISCENCES

OF

SCOTCH GROUSE MOORS.

MY grouse shooting days are now past. Increasing years and rheumatic muscles remind me that I have had my time, and a very good time too, so now let younger men take my place and profit by my experience, if it should so please them.

Let us look back on grouse shooting twenty-six years ago. Scotland, so far as regards the sporting of the far north, was then almost a *terra incognita*.

B

Railways ended at Inverness, and to get there needed a journey to Aberdeen, and from there by the slowest of slow railways, but quick enough—life was not run at so fast a pace as now.

The more remote districts of the north and west of Scotland were as unknown as the wilds of Labrador.

Previous to that time grouse shooting was for the few; we were content with our English shootings, and very nice and pleasant they were.

Every farmer, if the shooting was in his take, preserved his game; he shot it or he let it. The stubbles were long and full of weeds, the old pastures full of feg, and there was plenty of clover, but turnips not so much grown as now, excepting in the eastern counties, about which I know very little, the hedges and ditches not kept clean as they are now.

There was much less of hand rearing of pheasants; the hens were spared certainly the second time through, and nice mixed bags were made in covert with hares and rabbits and wild pheasants, hand rearing partridges being scarcely known.

Hares are now gone consequent on the Ground Game Act, and without them the farmer does not find it worth while to preserve, as the shooting will not let without ground game.

The open shooting was mostly done by two guns shooting together over dogs; in fact, you could not find your birds or fur without them.

How I made acquaintance with my first grouse was very funny; I will tell the tale:

I was at Scarborough with my wife and family, and,

talking shooting in the smoke room of the hotel, I was told as a great joke about the shooting on a moor of about 3000 acres near Pickering that was commonage, and free to anybody; of course, that was nonsense, the only parties having the rights of sporting were the commoners, and all others were trespassers; but that did not now matter, anybody shot upon it, but since then the commoners have been wise enough to join together and let the shooting rights at a very handsome rent.

Well, I was fired with the desire of seeing a grouse on the wing. It was rather slow for me at the seaside. I fancy that most paterfamilias find it so. Saying nothing, and cogitating the matter over, I determined to begin my first Twelfth, and accordingly I sent for a brace of my dogs from the south.

The shooting being free, it was necessary to be on the moor before daylight. Therefore I went over to Pickering by train in the afternoon of the eleventh, had some dinner at the inn, and hired a trap and man to drive me over, the driver to officiate as gilly or keeper, and, he being a Yorkshireman, anything in the way of sport could not come amiss to him. I found him keen as mustard to get me on the ground in good time, and at a good starting point.

With the first gleam of twilight the moor was ablaze with the fire of some thirty or more guns.

My first grouse was down before I could see him. Something fluttered up, I shot in the line, down came a bird, and to my intense delight I handled my first grouse—a fine old cock bird.

B 2

In three hours the whole thing was over, every bird not killed was put off on to neighbouring ground.

I had managed to get two and a half brace, and thought myself very lucky. I dare say a hundred brace were got off in that short three hours.

I took myself away to Saltersgate Inn, a comfortable wash up, some breakfast, and a nap, and in the afternoon quietly back to Pickering, and home to dinner.

That finished my grouse shooting for that season, but I had caught grouse fever.

The following season I joined some other men for a few days' shooting over dogs on a small moor in the county of Durham, and had a few pleasant enjoyable days, getting, perhaps, thirty brace in all. At that time grouse sat very fairly well to dogs for the first ten days in the English counties, as they now do in Perthshire and Aberdeenshire, but there was nothing like the quantity of birds on the English moors that there are now. One odd thing may be remarked: In all my sporting career I never shot but one curlew, and that was on this moor. Of birds, they are the wariest of the wary.

SEASON 1863.

The grouse fever was upon me at full fever heat, and I was determined that I would solve the problem of Scotch grouse shooting, and, finding in the spring of this season that an Aberdeen innkeeper advertised shooting, I wrote to him to know if he could put me in the way of a small place for one gun. Of course he replied glowingly, and said that a small moor by Gartly station, in Aberdeenshire, then on his hands, was quite enough for one gun, that capital lodgings were to be had at the merchant's house, and the price of the shooting for three weeks would be but £50.

I felt quite certain that I should be done, but I also knew that knowledge and experience could only be had by paying for it, so I plunged to what was not a very costly plunge, and accordingly I sent down my English keeper from Warwickshire.

In those days trains to Scotland did not afford the luxuries of to-day. Sleepers were unknown, and in the first-class carriage the elbow did not double up. The extreme of luxury was a second-class compartment retained for two men, and bed up the best way you could.

I was again at Scarborough. It was a slow, weary business to travel to York by a stopping train, and then the whole night and half next day getting to Aberdeen. So I bethought myself of asking the

London and Aberdeen S.S. Co. to take me off at Scarborough. This they agreed to do if I would lie off in the offing and wait for the boat.

I went off in the afternoon of the day. It was a fine day, fortunately, and I watched ship after ship, and at last, about 4 p.m., the big paddle wheels of the steamer loomed up.

It was the crack boat of the Aberdeen S.S. Co.; she had been chartered as a transport during the Crimean war, and was the only ship that rode out, or steamed out, the heavy gale off Balaclava that wrecked so many of our ships.

She tried to take me on board without a full stop, but I would not see it, and drifted a long way astern, causing considerable delay; but at last I was got up the side.

The captain swore great guns at the idea of stopping his ship for one passenger. I agreed with him, and recommended him to swear at his directors in London; and verily believe he would have sworn at them if he had had them there to swear at.

A smooth and lovely passage, arriving at Aberdeen about 11 a.m. next morning.

On arriving off the coast of Fife we ran through a school of whales, spouting and tumbling about in the most idiotic manner.

Arrived at Aberdeen I lunched at my friend the innkeeper's, who impressed me with the exceeding merits of my take, and the grouse I should get.

In the afternoon I was away by train to Gartly, and there found my keeper and dogs.

The lodgings were very plain, but good enough, and there, fortunately for me as turned out, also, lodging and shooting a moor rented from my innkeeper at Aberdeen, was that grand old sportsman the late Mr. Ginger Stubbs.

I am pretty certain that, my £50 being in view, that my bit of ground was cut off from Stubbs moor as an afterthought.

Mr. Stubbs was excellent company, and very good-naturedly he taught me a great many useful things that I desired to know about grouse shooting.

My moor was truly small: about an hour in the morning hunted it, and then I let it rest till the afternoon, giving birds time to work back home. The whole bag was about thirty brace of grouse, some grand brown hares, and a few sundries.

One of my dogs, never having been on grouse, until she saw them killed, took no more notice of them than she would of chickens.

A fortnight finished it, and I returned to England wiser in grouse lore than when I went. The £50 was well spent.

The novelty, the pure air, the heather hills, in fact, the whole thing, was delightful; it gave me a very considerable insight into grousing matters, and a knowledge of grouse moors in that locality, that was eventually of considerable use to me, and Stubbs put me right in many ways.

According to the fashion of the times I was shooting with a gun of 7¼lb. weight, and I was still further handicapping myself by holding my left hand too near the trigger guard.

"You shoot with too much gun," says Stubbs ; " push out your left hand along the barrels."

On my way south the Aberdeen innkeeper asked me to join a party that he was making up to attend the Highland sports that were to be held at Mar Lodge. I was nothing loth, and joined the party.

He took us down very comfortably along Dee side in a four horse omnibus, driven by himself, and gave me the box seat by his side. I think that he felt some compunction about the little do in respect to the moor " that was enough for one gun."

I forgave freely enough.

Everything was well arranged, rooms having been taken beforehand at the Hotel at Braemar.

The Prince and Princess of Wales were there (it was just after their marriage), and, of course, a great number of notables to meet them.

The whole affair was a large garden party; the railway being only open to Aberdeen, and the hotels in the locality not being so numerous or extensive as they are now, there was no crowding on the ground.

I did not care much for the sports, in fact, I never could see much in Highland sports, but other people do, so let them enjoy them, but my trip pleased me very much.

And so ended my first experience of Highland shooting.

———oo:o:co———

Season 1864.

In the spring I prepared for another campaign, I felt that I knew all about grouse moors and could take care of myself, but I had yet much to learn.

I enquired in all directions, and came across a gentleman who leased a large moor in Perthshire, the Glenshee moor, extending from the Spital of Glenshee to within a few miles of Braemar.

It was called 30,000 acres, probably might be 20,000.

The representations made to me were very good, and I was referred to a gentleman in Birmingham, who had shot there one or more seasons, and who quite truthfully gave me a very good account, so far as his experience went.

The moor was shot by four guns, shooting in two parties, I took one gun at £100, finding my share of dogs, ponies, gillies, &c., and I very naturally congratulated myself that I was well landed, and could not be otherwise than in for a good thing, and safe from all pitfalls left open for the unwary.

There was no lodge in Glenshee in those days, and it had to be shot from the Spital Inn.

The guns had to ride ponies from three to eight miles to get to their beats, men and dogs walking on beforehand, so that nearly half the time and labour was taken up in travelling to and fro', but as it turned out it did not matter much.

The moor was a fine moor, with fine heather, but with too much green ground upon it.

It included some of the high Grampians, and marched with the Mar Forest on the one end, and with Caen Lochan Forest on the east side.

For those who cared to climb 3000 feet and more, and risk sprained limbs on the roughest of broken rocks and boulders, there was a fair sprinkling of ptarmigan.

I was fairly well dogged, I had my brace of dogs, and beforehand on faith I had bought a middle aged pointer bitch from the keeper for £5, and a very good purchase she was; later on I bred some very good puppies from her and my dog Rap, and in addition to her I had my brace of dogs and my English keeper to complete my team.

We all reached the Spital, hiring from Blairgowrie, a day or two before the 12th, in high spirits and hopes for the coming fray.

The morning after our arrival my keeper came to me with a very long face, he had got it from the gillie that we were done, fairly done brown, that there was literally nothing on the ground. The moor was very high, nothing under 1500 feet above the sea, rising to 3000 feet, the limit of heather, and a severe snow storm late on in the spring had killed the young birds and driven down the old ones to lower ground, the lower moors below us were full of birds.

I was very down in the mouth. I had, as I thought, taken every precaution, and was also rather full of my cleverness at getting into what I took to be so good a thing, and had bragged considerably; but at the same time would scarcely credit that such an extent of fine ground could hold nothing. I said nothing, but waited for the outcome.

On the morning of the Twelfth we went through the usual routine of ponies, panier ponies, gillies, dogs, &c., returning at night with a dozen brace of old birds amongst us, perhaps not so many.

The next day the same farce was enacted on another side of the moor, with worse results.

That night there was a great talk of what could be done with deer. In October, perhaps, something might be done, but in August they were well kept in by the Mar and Caen Lochan Foresters, and the talk ended where it began.

After that my keeper and I scrambled about on the high hills, after ptarmigan, an odd grouse, a hare or two. One day I managed to get six brace of ptarmigan and some dotterel—and very pretty birds they were.

Ptarmigan are curious birds on the Glenshee hills, the ground being so desperately rough it needed all your wits to walk and take care of your gun, marking down the birds as they fluttered up like pigeons.

It was useless to shoot at a bird unless you could make sure to kill him outright, as the wounded birds crept into holes amongst the rocks like rabbits.

When the birds were marked down you got to them the best way you could, and had to look very sharp to distinguish them from the colour of the stones as they crept about.   You would then shoot one on the ground, and take another as they rose.

The old cock birds in their summer plumage were very handsome birds.

I soon had enough, and in about a fortnight made tracks for the south.

But before going south I suggested to the boss of the shooting, who had let me the gun, that, as he must have known before he let it what the state of things would be, he should, anyhow, return one half the money, and that more especially as there was one corrie that held birds, and, at the solicitation of the keeper, I had let them alone, being the only breeding stock left to him, but I could make nothing of him. One of the other guns, whom I will call Fred, and who had shot there several seasons, also pressed the matter sharply, but his blandishments were of no effect, and Fred was so annoyed that he said he would shoot there no more, and would be glad to join with me in taking a place, if we could find one pretty accessible, that would carry two guns shooting together.

In those days there were practically no agents, in the modern acceptance of the term, excepting Snowie, of Inverness.   There were, also, very few advertisements, and accessible moors were in no great plenty, and such as there were, were let to permanent tenants, who renewed their leases at the old rents; in fact, it was pretty much the rule that so long as the old tenant choose to remain there should be no rise of rent.   Times were then easy with landowners, and they were easy with their tenants.

SEASON 1865.

I kept a careful watch over the advertisements in the *Field* and other papers, and in the spring I noted the following advertisement on a certain Saturday :

" To be let, the Shootings of Glenmarkie, in Aberdeenshire and Banffshire, extending over 11,000 acres of moor and low ground ; references to last tenant. Application to be made to Mr. Snowie, of Inverness, or the Law Agents in Edinburgh."

I did not sleep upon it, but wrote that night to my law agents in Edinburgh, asking them to call first thing on Monday morning upon the advertisers, and telegraph me the rent and the name of last tenant. The reply was prompt ; the late tenant was Mr. Thos. Powell, of Newport, Mon. ; proprietors, the Fife Trustees ; the rent, £265. I telegraphed immediately to a mutual friend at Newport, and received my reply on the Tuesday morning by letter.

Mr. Powell reported that it was a capital moor, with splendid birds, and lots of them, but needed to be shot quickly, as they packed early ; that, in addition to grouse, there were a great number of large brown hares on the lower beats, but that he could say nothing about the partridges and snipe on the low ground as he had never troubled with them.

Mr. Powell had given up the place to take some very large deer forest, but that did not satisfy him, and some of my readers will probably remember that not very long afterwards, whilst on a shooting expedition after big game in Abyssinia, accompanied by his wife and family, the whole party were massacred.

Fred knew the moor perfectly well at second hand through a friend who had shot upon it a few years previously, and two years before at Gartly I had gathered information about this identical moor, so, without delay, by 10 a.m. on Tuesday morning, I had telegraphed my Edinburgh agents to close a seven years lease at £265, which, as my agents could satisfy the proprietors' agents as to my eligibility as a tenant, was at once agreed to, and so Fred and I were joined in what proved a very pleasant partnership.

To illustrate the keenness for really good places in those days at the moderate rents at which things went, a Staffordshire gentleman had written on the Saturday for particulars of the moor, and was replied to in due course on the Monday.

He accepted by letter on the Tuesday, but by telegraph I had instructed my agents to conclude the matter, and was thus before him.

Having taken the shooting, the next best thing was to go and look at it.

The bulk of the grouse ground was in Banff, and extended over about 7000 acres, including 1000 acres adjoining, that we rented at £15 a year from a neighbouring proprietor.

In addition to the grouse ground there was about

3000 acres of rough hills, partly in gorse, bracken, broom, patches of heather, and rough pastures.

This rough ground carried a goodly number of grouse, beside snipe, golden plover, brown hares, and some few rabbits.

The low ground consisted of about 2000 acres of small arable farms prettily mixed up with the rough ground and the lower beats of the moorland.

There were enormous brown hares everywhere excepting on the higher grouse beats.

The moorland was full of grouse, and the heather splendid, but had not been sufficiently and judiciously burnt.

One hill side of about 1500 acres, nearly a fourth of the grouse ground, was deep old heather all in one patch, without a break in it.

It was frightfully dangerous in case of fire, as the whole would have swept away in one terrific blaze.

It was late in the season, but at once we put in two belts of burning, dividing it into four, and the next season burnt it properly in strips, improving the feeding and nesting ground.

On the one side we were bounded by the river Deveron, and there was salmon fishing, but they were late, and as red as mahogany, and also very stiff to rise ; in fact, the few that we had were taken with the worm in the rocky pools, so the salmon fishings were very little worth. The trout fishing was not much account, though in the month of May fair baskets could be made during the rise of the March brown.

The lodge was small but well enough situated, just

seven miles from Huntley. As a matter of course the windows looked on to the wrong point of view, but that is almost always the case in the older shooting lodges. There was a small but very productive garden between the lodge and the river; at end of August and beginning of September the bush fruit and the strawberries were splendid.

The situation of the lodge by the river side was very pleasant, and made gay by flowering annuals, which were much brighter in colour than those grown in the south.

We were very fortunate in the minister, who was a gentleman and a scholar, and we liked the schoolmaster.

Little more than a stone's throw from the manse was a salmon pool, and regularly after breakfast and after tea, no matter the state of water or weather, our old minister fished the pool once up and once down, it might take him five to ten minutes.

He was very reticent as to his success, but our impression was that he had about a fish a week the season through—of course he would fish blank during drought, but he fished away all the same.

Our next door neighbour was Beldornie, with its little old fashioned castle, a habitable castle, and let as the lodge for the Beldornie shooting, and the banks of the river between our lodge and the castle were pretty steep and beautifully wooded with natural hazel, birch and ash.

The kennels were pretty good, and as Fred and I shot together, three or four brace of dogs did us well.

Ready for the Start.

We were well dogged for the 12th, with my three dogs and three of Fred's; one of his was a queer beast, a rough-looking rugged Russian setter. He was honest, staunch, and industrious, and quartered his ground well, but nothing would stop him, you might whistle and whistle till you were hoarse until he got into the neighbourhood of birds, and then down he sat on his rump and would wait, aye an hour if need be. Very rarely did he spring birds, as he did not draw upon them until you were with him. On one occasion so far did he go that we uncoupled another dog and worked up to him, getting birds on the way until we attended to his.

Fred and his wife and I went down a few days before the 12th, and he and I had a skirmishing afternoon on part of the rough ground, getting brown hare, snipe, plover, and a rabbit or two.

The grouse ground was in six beats, but on the 12th we went through some of the rough ground, getting thirty-one brace of magnificent birds and some brown hares and sundries, and the next day on a grouse beat about sixty brace, and continued to make good bags for several days, when the weather broke and quickly pulled the joint bags down to thirty and twenty brace a day.

We made about 370 brace, besides a lot of brown hares and sundries, returning south early in September to commence partridge shooting about the 10th of September, which is early enough in most English counties.

To get off a large bag would have needed two more

C

guns shooting in another party, and so take off all that was possible in the first week before the birds began to pack, but we were happy enough, and did not care to cram the little lodge too full.

To show how very ticklish the birds were, shooting four days a week, it would take ten days to get over the beats once, and during our lease we never remember getting over the six beats before a break of weather and the birds packing.

We carried our game, lunches, spare ammunition, &c., on a pannier pony, Our pony man, Geordie Gordon, was a character—he was Jack of all trades, minister's man, clerk to the kirk, and pony man in the shooting season, and also did what gardening was needed, his dialect the purest Aberdeen, so pure that I always needed an interpreter. He was expected to keep his eyes upon and mark wide birds. On one occasion a bird towered—" Where did he go, did you mark him, Geordie?" "Yes, yes, up, up, up—up there," said Geordie, pointing to the sky.

SEASON 1866.

This season we added three puppies of Nell and Rap's to the kennel; they were liver and white like the old dogs, so we called the family Mr. and Mrs. Rap, and the young Raps, but though the puppies turned out well, none of them came up to old Rap. He would do anything, point, retrieve, catch rats, rabbiting, or anything you liked.

He would do what not one dog in twenty, aye! in fifty, will do: if he had a slant wind of birds he turned back and took a round swing to get his wind properly; with most dogs you have to whistle and work them round by hand.

I bred him from a pure heavy Spanish pointer dog and a well-bred English bitch, but one so rank that her owner gave her to me to breed from, and then make away with her. I kept three puppies out of the litter, but, excepting Rap, although better looking, they were no good—no real work in them. They would have sold well, but I preferred to shoot them to selling the man who would have bought them.

One other very good looking likely puppy I gave to the old Marquis de la ——, but I believe, as the old gentleman made a pet of him, and endowed him with a collar and bells, and would have shaved him had he had anything to shave, that his sporting career was not brilliant.

C 2

I came by Rap's father rather oddly : he belonged to a working carpenter, who had picked up the puppy at some nobleman's place where he had been working, had broken him well, and he was a very careful, slow ranger, the very thing for English shooting in the days of stubbles, and I had had my eye upon him all the early summer, and at last, about the middle of August, I negociated the purchase for £7 ; but the dog never came, and I could not get to hear anything about him. But in the afternoon of August 31 up comes Mr. Carpenter and his dog to "implement" the bargain, as Scotch people would say. I wanted to know how the delay came about, and, after a lot of cross-questioning, it came out that General ——'s coachman and he had agreed that the dog was to be planted on the general at £12, and the difference of £5 to be divided between coachman and carpenter; but the planting did not come off, so in the eleventh hour he was brought up to me, and I was glad to take him.

As Shot, the Spanish dog, grew old, he became very dodgy; he had the run of the house, and would get away and hunt the hedges for the labourer's dinners and bring them home, napkins and all ; and, if taken into the town to the butcher's shop, he would go, and, somehow or other, get away unperceived with a piece of meat. He was never caught red handed, at any rate by the butcher, who was consequently accused of base slander.

The staunchness of those Spanish pointers was remarkable. On one occasion he was pointing and roading, and pointing a landrail in a patch of clover; the bird was headed and rose, and flew right towards the dog's mouth. Shot opened his mouth, and closed it on the bird, and then he stood stock still without moving a muscle.

He never attempted to meddle with game or rabbits, but if he came near a tiny rabbit just out of the burrow he would pick him up and bolt him like a pill.

This was a very good season, the second day getting over 100 brace to the two guns, shooting together over the same dogs—getting in all about 400 brace in the season, besides hares and sundries.

But Fred, when we left the place, was full of fear and trembling, as at the latter end we got two or three badly-diseased birds. Fred knew what disease meant; but to me it was something new yet to learn; and, looking at the magnificent stock of fine healthy birds, I made light of his fears.

When we took the place, and afterwards went down to look at it, every inquiry was made as to disease, but not a soul would own to anything. It was stated on all hands that on Glenmarkie disease was a thing unknown, but Fred did not believe in its being so. I daresay many of my readers have been told the same flattering tale about other moors, and with the same results.

Before leaving we discharged the keeper; we could not do with his domineering ways, and, after careful inquiry, we engaged young David Black, a son of a keeper of Lord Airlie's. He came of a good game keeping stock, and was all that we could wish for.

He was married to an Orkney woman; we liked them both, and they have been in my service ever since, which should speak well for master and man.

SEASON 1867.

This was indeed a disastrous season; it was really frightful. Fred's worst fears were more than realised. In the spring disease raged with intense virulence, dead birds lying about in scores on the green ground by the waterside and elsewhere—many in full plumage and apparently in full health. Before the 12th, with the exception of a few broods on the rough ground, there was practically, so to speak, not a bird left upon the grouse ground.

The whole district was in the same condition; and it goes without saying that we did not go near the place. Fred said, gloomily enough, " There will be no grouse shooting for three years," and he was practically right.

David Black reported that the spates on the river brought down dead birds in such quantities as to choke the surface of the eddies and backwaters.

I was almost in despair; I was very keen on the shooting, and I had struggled hard for five years to get it, and realised but two good seasons out of the five.

SEASON 1868.

Of course, we let the grouse alone for this season, as well as in 1867. There were very few to let alone ; but the disease was gone, and we comforted ourselves the best way we could with the low-ground shooting in October.

David Black had worked up the low ground well. When we first took the place there were very few partridges. The first season there was a covey of twenty-two birds close to the lodge. We let them alone, and they had multiplied, and in addition there were also a few odd pairs in other parts of the ground. We had shot none, and they had had three years jubilee and pretty good breeding seasons.

In these high, stormy countries, during heavy snows the poor things can get very little food, and naturally draw down into the stackyards for food and shelter, and, if not carefully looked after, get potted by the farmer, but are not of much good to him, as they are little better than skin and bone.

Black looked after them. I don't think that our former keeper troubled himself, or the stock would have got up quicker ; and there was now a fine stock of all sorts of low-country game, pheasants excepted. Of course, by a fine stock I mean a fine stock for a wild stormy country.

We had a most enjoyable fortnight's shooting over

dogs. In the twelve days we managed to make a mixed bag of 600 head—partridge, snipe, plover, brown hares, rabbits, &c.

The grouse we let alone, except a stray old cock now and again that had survived through the epidemic— very handsome to look at, but, like the monarch of the glen, very tough, and unsavoury on the table.

Of course, on that wild ground the covies of partridges were, looking at the extent of ground, few and far between.

The dogs hunted the small turnip fields and the ground round the edges of the oat stubbles, say, for a hundred yards about. It might be wooded burn sides, or deep feg or heather, and, perhaps, whins and broom. The birds took a lot of finding. Of course, we got other stuff, meanwhile, on the way; and the covey once found, and flushed again and again in neaps, brackens, heather, or what not, the dogs kept pegging them until the covey was pretty well cleared up. Sometimes a covey would utterly beat us by settling into heavy patches of gorse that the dogs would not face—at any rate, not work properly; and as to walking them up with a retriever, they would run about, but knew better than to flush.

After that very naturally we went down every October until the end of the lease, and the last season we had 190 brace of partridges alone.

When hunting near the moor edges we often got a few grouse that were down to the stubble; and in these delightful mixed bags over dogs, how a couple of brace of fine grouse were appreciated.

These mixed bags in the crisp October air, the walking, the variety of sport, though not the quantity, beat the August shooting for enjoyment of sport. You would not know what the dog's point might mean; it might in some ground be hare, snipe, partridge, or grouse. I have made doubles at hare and snipe. The hares were splendid. You may not believe it, but Fred made a double at hares that weighed 22lb. the brace.

One season I stopped over for an extra day by myself—it would be the 18th of October—on the rough ground, and made the following mixed bag over dogs:

    4 Grouse, stalked on the plough from behind the
        dykes.
    6 Partridges.
    2 Woodcock (very unusual).
    4 Snipe.
    9 Brown hares.
    2 Golden plover.
    1 Green plover.
    1 Rabbit.
    ——
    29 Head.

Grouse, when they get on the plough, are sometimes very stupid, in the above case I stalked the four birds, there were but four; I shot one on the ground, did not show myself, let the bird lie; the others then just fluttered up and flew fifty yards; and down within reach of the dyke, got another, then the other two again fluttered up and down again, that time I jumped up and showed myself and got the pair right and left as they rose.

SEASON 1869.

Black said that we might go down in August and stretch our legs, and kill a few grouse on the rough ground, so down we went, and made about sixty brace of grouse and a lot of sundries, especially golden plover. Of these there were quantities, and in ordinary August months we were far too busy with grouse to heed them.

One afternoon a pack of green and a pack of golden plover were very busy fighting and screaming for the possession of a hill side, and so busy that they took little or no heed of us, and four barrels dropped twelve couple, of course, some of the cripples needed another barrel.

There is one way, and an almost certain way of circumventing flocks of golden plover: they are very inquisitive birds, you will see them on the face of the hill, mostly small round hills; let the keeper sit down with the dogs, say 100 yards in front of them, and whilst they are watching him, slip quietly round the hill, over the top, down on the flock before they are aware of you, and a family shot into the brown with two barrels of No. 8 will sometimes bring down two or three couple.

We had a good deal of trouble with fellows coming up from Huntly, fishing. Powell had let anybody come, and it was difficult to stop it. One morning we saw a young fellow putting a salmon rod together on the other side of the river, I sent over the under keeper, Sandy, a big, strong Highlander, to put him off; but he would not budge, he stated that we were going out for our sport, shooting, and he meant to have his sport, fishing. Sandy was again sent over to intimate that if he fished he was to take his rod and put him personally into the salmon pool. " What, take my rod and put me in the river, contrary to law?" Sandy simply said he had no option, it was the master's orders, and he took the rod as a beginning. I was summoned for illegally taking the rod, and took out a counter summons for the fishing, each party was fined by the sheriff, the fisher much heavier than we were, but my decisive action stopped all further trouble. If I had not taken the rod I should not have got the fellow's name.

Season 1870.

Three years weary patience was rewarded in the fourth year with a fine grouse season, and, not being quite so thick upon the ground as in ordinary good seasons, the grouse sat better, and in the second and third weeks we made better bags than was customary.

Our lease was running out, this was the sixth season.

The factor did his best to induce us to renew for another seven years. I was anxious to do so, notwithstanding our disappointments, but my chum did not seem to care to do it, and I hardly liked to do so without him, and very much I afterwards regretted it.

The factor had always used us well, in the best possible manner, he had an old-fashioned notion that decent folks who paid a good round sum for sport and gave no trouble, were entitled to consideration, and to have something for their money ; the modern factor quite discards ideas so very ridiculous.

In the spring of this season I was down with my second son for some trout fishing in the river, and we had some pleasant sport, being favoured with two or three small rises of water and a good show of March browns. We managed to make nice little baskets of 6lb. to 7lb. each on most days, fishing the Beldornie water as well as our own.

We had, neither of us, ever seen a red deer—anyhow, on his native heath—and we decided to make a day out to Glen Fiddoch Forest.

We knew that it was five miles across the Glen-markie ground to the extreme point of our outside march at Auchendown Castle, and how much further we knew not. That, bear in mind, was before the days of ordnance maps.

We were all good walkers, that is, David and myself, and my son Oliver ; he held a front place in athletics at Rugby School.

We crossed the moor south of Auchendown, and then got at last on to the road track to Glen Fiddoch Lodge. Altogether, it was a long tramp, the last few miles following up the Fiddoch burn, but time and labour at last landed us at the lodge.

The lodge was very old-fashioned, was all on the ground floor, with rooms on one side of a long building, and a passage on the other side.

The housekeeper was a civil old body : would give us some tea, which we appreciated, and made much of us in every way ; showed us the room that had been used by the Queen the year before, when visiting the Duke. Everthing was simple in the extreme. I am sure that no broker would have bid over eighteen pence for the washing stand in the Queen's bedroom.

On our way we saw deer by scores on the hill sides, and also round the lodge.

All was very pleasant up to now, but there was the walk back. By the time we reached Auchendown we had had enough, and there was the five miles across heavy moorland yet to be done. Some people say that your native heath, and the springiness of the heather, make walking pleasant and easy, but don't believe it; my notion has always been that one mile of moorland is equal to two on the hard road.

David was fairly done. It is not the first time that I had walked down the natives, both in Ireland and in Scotland, but I never expected to see David brought to a stand.

Well, we laid down and rested a good hour, refreshed with biscuits and whiskey and water, and put the five miles behind us before dark.

Season 1871.

The proprietor, to our very great surprise and astonishment, intimated to us and to the tenants of the arable farms on the Fife estates, that, on the expiration of the current sporting leases, they should have the right to kill ground game on their arable farms, how and when they liked.

This was a knock down blow. I am inclined to think that the factor had an inkling of it when he pressed us to renew; that he wanted to make his sporting leases safe, so that they should not be affected by it.

There were forty tenants in Glenmarkie who would have the right to shoot, and, naturally, I did not see my way to preserve game on the low ground in the teeth of that, so, with great reluctance, we told our good factor that we should have to go.

He offered considerable reduction in rent—anything to induce us to stop, except rescinding the ground game fad, and that he could not do.

The only reason that could have suggested such action on the part of the proprietor must have been political, probably to outbid M'Combie, the Radical candidate for Aberdeenshire; but so it was, and there was no way of getting over it.

The stock of grouse upon the ground was very large,

and the late Mr. O. joined us in the grouse time, and after the first two days he and Fred shot together.

In the first two days shooting together Fred and I made over the same dogs over one hundred brace a-day. The total bag in the two days was two hundred and ten brace of grouse, and some sundries; and I have but little doubt that, if I had been bent on a swagger bag, shooting by myself, commencing at 8 a.m. in place of 11 a.m., I could have made a hundred brace in one day to my own gun.

After that I managed the birds pretty well by myself, and when they became skittish, by starting about from 12 to 1 o'clock, and hunting the wild ground into good sitting ground, taking time for lunch, and beginning to work the birds about 3 to 4 o'clock, I made pretty shooting.

I had to work the dog myself, the gillie keeping down in the heather out of sight.

Old Rap was gone, I hope to where good dogs go, for he deserved it if dogs can deserve it.

His two sons, Duke and Prince, did my work. Duke was a nice-mannered, tractable, gentle beast, but Prince was a rank tartar.

So soon as you loosed him from the couples, he would do some rank trick, get on the foot of a hare, or what not; then come in to the whip, get it hot, wag his tail, and then for some time go to work with a skill and courage far beyond Duke, then again to the whip, and so he went on to the end of his days.

One afternoon I had a laughable sell—the laugh was against me, though. My chums were not going out, so I drove my birds carefully into sitting ground, that was principally on what was their beat.

I got a fine lot of birds into good ground, and at 3 p.m. rose up from lunch to make what I knew would be a good afternoon's work, rather out of the common.

As I got up, who should I see but David and the two chums coming round the shoulder of the hill, into the ground I had carefully filled with birds. They had point after point, and made an unexpectedly fine afternoon's shooting, about twenty-five brace of birds. They had not the slightest notion how it came about. I said nothing, not I, as I had rather stretched a point by driving into their beat, but David knew that something had been done to get them this good shooting, and worked it out of my gillie after we got home, and a pretty laugh there was, and no thanks.

Of course I got no shooting that afternoon ; perhaps a brace or two before lunch, and a brace or two after.

It was a charming season ; exceptionally nice weather, no gales, plenty of sun, and just enough rain to keep things pleasant and scent good.

My own bag was three hundred and ninety-one and a-half brace, and one hundred and fourteen brace of partridges in October, besides a lot of brown hares, plover, snipe, &c.

Altogether we had a good way over six hundred brace, and a special good time with the low ground in October.

The snipe shooting was far better in the earlier years of our lease. It was, indeed, very good,

D

especially in one swamp of a few acres, that was too soft for cattle to tread it, and there the snipe bred in large quantities; but an enterprising farmer came along with some large pipe drains, and settled the snipe. It was a sad pity, but you cannot hammer into proprietors that the value of the snipe shooting far exceeds the couple of pounds extra value of grazing caused by draining, in fact, that snipe shooting would with some men be the turning point of whether they took the shooting or not.

It was getting time to look about me for another shooting, and, making enquiries, I had the offer of a celebrated moor not far away, up in Strathspey.

The moor was noted for swagger bags on the first few days, so I sent David to inspect and report, which he did faithfully and fully. It was a grand place, and the rent moderate.

He was given every information, and shown the game books with a record of twenty-five years (that takes us back in the records of disease for nearly half-a-century). On the average, it showed but three good seasons out of seven.

I was very much surprised. and I did not feel inclined to face that, but many to whom money is no object, and who can shoot elsewhere as well, would say, " Yes, we will pay seven years' rent and expenses for three years of extraordinary sport in the three good seasons." It ended in my declining it.

Some two or three years previously I had been in Caithness for a fortnight's salmon fishing at the end of

Braal Castle.

February, on the Thurso. If I remember rightly, Mr. R. L. Price had given me his rod on the river for that time.

Then, at Braal Castle I made the acquaintance of William Dunbar, an acquaintance that lasted so long as Dunbar lived, and still continues with his widow, and his daughter, Mrs. Sutherland.

Dunbar was a very remarkable man in his way. He made his living by taking shootings and fishings from Caithness proprietors.

Acting under his advice, the proprietor opened up the main strath, by making a road from the county road at Strathmore, past Dalnawillan and Glutt, to join the road at Braemore on to Dunbeath, and so open up access to Glutt and Dalnawillan from the south, without going round by Wick or Thurso.

He also built Strathmore and Dalnawillan lodges and keepers' houses, kennels, &c.

Dunbar leased from the proprietor the whole of the fishings and shootings from the sea to the Sutherland march, and in addition many smaller shootings in the Wick and Watton districts from other proprietors, who all knew little or nothing about sporting subjects (and, as a matter of fact, they and their factors know as little now), still less how to make them available for, and how to introduce them to, southern sportsmen. As it was, Dunbar was really a perfect godsend to the various proprietors, and to the county of Caithness generally, from the large sums of money brought into the county by his shooting and fishing friends and tenants.

The Ulbster shootings, which constituted the main

strath when I first knew Dunbar, were divided as follows, or thereabouts, including about· 5000 acres leased from other proprietors :—

Braal	10,000
Strathmore and Achlybster ...	19,000
Chullacan and Bachlas ...	6,000
Dalnawillan	18,000
Glutt ... ,..	15,000
	68,000

The Thurso salmon angling was let to six rods, and the anglers lodged in the early months at Braal Castle, and later on at Strathmore Lodge.

In those days the lower beats fished well in February and March, the fish running from 8lb. to 10lb., with an occasional big one; but now in the early months they run about double the weight, few and far between, and make up almost at once for Loch More and the upper beats. The reason for the change is not far to seek.

Dunbar had a happy knack in letting shootings and fishings. He understood sport, was frank, truthful, and kept back nothing. It did not need an old hand to read between the lines of his statements.

He was pretty keen in making his bargains, but once made he did his best to make things comfortable for his clients. He went for a connection, and he made one. There was not a grain of meanness or littleness in his composition ; whether in the bond or not he did the fair thing. He knew how to deal with gentlemen, and men felt safe in his hands, and voids in his shootings and fishings were rare.

He was popular in Caithness with all classes.

Fred elected not to continue grouse shooting, and our pleasant partnership came to an end, and I had to decide what I would do.

When in Caithness, I had picked up all the information I could gather as to Caithness moors.

In all ways they were the very opposite to Glenmarkie. Grouse sat well for quite a month, rather more on the hill moors, and rather less on the low moors, and nowhere did they pack, except in heavy snowstorms when the ground was all white, and they made away to the lower grounds for food.

There was nothing like the quantity of grouse that I had at Glenmarkie, but the ranges were larger—wide ranging dogs and good walking imperative; but when dogs got birds they sat well.

There was also a considerable quantity of wild fowl, wild geese, ducks, and blue hares; very few on Glenmarkie. No low ground shooting, in fact, no arable on the hill moors.

The heather was short and stunted, with stretches of deer grass and flows; in fact, no good heather on the hill moors. Excepting on the burn banks and dry knolls, the ground was mostly peat bog, too sot to carry a pannier pony, and the birds had, to be carried in panniers on gillies' backs.

The trout fishing in the upper streams and burns of the Thurso that fed Loch More was pretty good. The

trout were plentiful but small, running about four to
the pound, but they came quick and lively.   The loch
fishing was not much account; perhaps I should except
òne loch, that yielded heavy trout of fine quality, but
very shy.

Glenmarkie was a Christian-like place, but the
principal moors of Caithness were a howling wilderness, not a tree and scarcely a shrub; but it was a
wilderness of weird beauty in changing lights.   The
outlook from the top of Ben Alasky on a wild stormy
day, with changing sunlight and storms, over the loch
bespattered land, backed up by the cliffs of Orkney,
was one of the things to see and to remember.
    To me this wild and weird land has great charms.
    Well, I wrote to Dunbar in the early summer to say
that my lease was expiring, and that I wanted a
shooting for 1872, and on a long lease.
    He offered me one or two small ones in the Watton
and Wick districts, but I told him that I must have
Glutt, Dalnawillan, or Strathmore.   He replied that
all were let on lease, and could not be had.
    But in September he wrote again, saying that his
tenant Col. C., from failing health, desired probably
to relinquish the lease of Dalnawillan and Chullacan,
18,000 and 6000 acres respectively, and that they
could be had jointly or separately at £400 and £160,
for the unexpired term of the Colonel's lease, of which
there was nine years then to run.
    I sent Black down to inspect and report.
    It culminated as Dunbar had foreshadowed, and at

the latter end of October I went straight from Glen-markie to Dalnawillan.

The railway was then open to Helmsdale, and from there I travelled by mail coach as far as Dunbeath, a lovely drive past Berriedale, the property of the Duke of Portland, but being night I could see but little of it on that occasion.

I slept at Dunbeath, and posted over next morning, 16 miles, the whole distance across the moorland, to Dalnawillan.

Angus Mackay, the Colonel's gillie, met me at the march with a dog, and, getting the gun out of the case, I shot up to the lodge.

The day was warm and sunny, and I was amazed and puzzled; I saw no birds. At Glenmarkie they would have rolled up over the sky line; but birds sat to the dog, and I killed three and a half brace. Three days before, at Glenmarkie, being the last day that I should shoot, I tried to get a few grouse, my endeavours resulting in one bird, but plenty of packs rising before me.

The next day was showery and gusty, and the birds did not sit well, but at Glenmarkie they would have rolled up in packs.

I spent two nights at the lodge with the Colonel's brother, who came over to meet me, and next morning was away to Thurso to meet the Colonel and Dunbar.

It was agreed that the lease should be assigned. I suggested a new lease from Dunbar, and that he should make it the full ten years.

" Take it to the end of my lease, seventeen years,

if you like," says Dunbar, to which I assented; so it was settled that I should take the 24,000 acres of Dalnawillan, and Chullacan, and Backlas, at the rent of £560, proprietor paying all rates and taxes, and I paying my keeper and all other expenses.

This included a joint right of trout fishing on Dalnawillan, Strathmore, and Glutt, and salmon fishing, after June 1.

When I returned to England my shooting friends told me that I was crazy to take shooting in such an out-of-the-way, wild country, and tie myself up for such a term of years. I felt I had done right; I meant grouse shooting and fishing, and that, as railways had crept up, and were creeping up, that shootings were more likely to improve than get worse, in case of some unforeseen event occurring that should cause me to cease to shoot.

Black had made every inquiry as to disease. Dunbar told me plump that five years before they had had disease, but it was a mild attack, and did not stop shooting. As, however, the moor had not carried a good head of grouse until the year I took it, I expect that the tenants shot away, killing down the breeding stock that should have been nursed. It was admitted that the moors on the south and east had been badly hit with disease.

I took the place with my eyes open, and was prepared to take the fat with the lean, but I candidly confess that I had more lean than I expected or liked.

I looked for disease in 1874, but it came sooner.

SEASON 1872.

Of course, the moor was larger than I needed for my own personal use, and according to the fashion of the time I proposed to get others to join me, so I looked out for a couple of guns to share expenses.

It was proposed that the moor should be shot in three parties of one gun each.   There was no difficulty in those days in getting guns to join, but it is very difficult now.   I take it, that before the passing of the Ground Game Act there was more English shooting of a moderate character, and, so to speak, men were educated to shoot, and naturally were desirous of trying their hands on grouse ; besides, the shooting squires are not so well to do throughout the country as they were before the depression in land.

I advertised in the *Field* on a Saturday, and before Monday was over a gentleman in Berkshire had been straight to my place in Shropshire and arranged for one gun, and the other was fixed before the end of the week.   Very nice, cheery, gentlemenly men they both were.   Mr. C. and Mr. D. were my colleagues.

My wife, my sister-in-law, and the children, accompanied us in August ; we had a sleeping saloon as far as Helmsdale, the then terminus of Northern Railways.

That night we stopped at Ross's Hotel.   Helmsdale was the only entrance by road into Caithness, and Ross's the only hotel, so the capacity of Ross's rooms was the gauge of the traffic. The Countess of Caithness had our rooms the night before, and they were booked for somebody else the night after us.

The next day Ross posted us in a *char-a-banc* the thirty-two miles to Dalnawillan, stopping to lunch and bait horses at Dunbeath; the luggage had gone on before in two carts.

The drive to Dunbeath was lovely over the Ord and past Berriedale, the Duke of Portland's place.

At Dunbeath after lunch the party walked down to the sea to look at the rocks and fishing boats, and we all enjoyed it thoroughly; after this break there was a sixteen mile drive across the moorland, passing Braemore and Glutt Lodges on the left.

There being no railway we made arrangements with the Glutt party, and engaged with a carrier to bring letters, supplies, &c., from Dunbeath and take back game bags, 'empties, &c., the following day. We were quite as well off, in fact, better than if we had been fidgetted with railway, post-office, and telegraph at our elbow.

Things went well with us, the shooting was excellent, the Chullacan and Backlas beats were especially full of birds that season. At Chullacan was a very primitive farmhouse with a small cooking place, and a room for us to serve as sitting-room and bedroom. The farmer's room was at the other end of the house, and in his case the smoke found its way through the hole in the roof. At this place we lodged twice for two nights, each time when we shot the beats on that side. We were pretty cramped, making up three small beds at night; the morning bath we took by standing outside the house in a state of nature while the gillies douched us with pails of cold spring water.

The first time that we went over on the three days shooting, I made forty-two, forty, and forty-five brace to my own shoulder, and on our return we enjoyed the comfort of a day's lazy rest amongst the comforts of Dalnawillan Lodge. We were all very happy, my two chums in raptures, and insisting on engaging their guns for the next season.

Man proposes, God disposes.

Bag.	Dalnawillan and Rumsdale.
Grouse	1098 brace.
Sundries	67½ ,,

The birds were healthy in a way when we left, but did not look well in plumage. It had been a wet draggly summer, and that partly accounted for it; but before leaving we saw a few very seedy birds on our Dunbeath march.

Dunbar had been very busy all the season for the Duke of Sutherland.

At that time the shootings and fishings of the Helmsdale Strath were divided into three great lumps of ground :

Sir John Karslake the upper end, say about	60,000 acres.
Mr. Hadwen, the middle, say about	60,000 ,,
Mr. Meredith, the bottom end, say about	60,000 ,,

I cannot be precise about the extent, but that was about it.

Mr. Akroyd's, in Strath Naver, was almost unlimited, and included nearly all the salmon fishing of the Naver.

The Duke was disturbed in his mind, or somebody else was, and, Dunbar being the only man who really knew anything about the management of shootings and fishings, the Duke sent for him and engaged his services to report on the whole matter of the Sutherland shootings and fishings for the handsome fee of £1000, and well earned too, as he was the only man that could do it.

Acting under his advice the Duke divided the Helmsdale Strath into six shootings, with six salmon rods on the river, one rod to each shooting at £50 for those who chose to take them, and so the thing remains to this day, but with rents increased and half the ground taken away, the then existing tenants were somewhat indignant, but there was nothing much to grumble about.

Mr. Hadwen, who lived upon his place, being very little away, and also farmed the sheep, had built himself a good house on a yearly tenancy, went to see the Duke and the factor, Mr. Peacock, and they had a meeting about it.

"Your grace, I have been your tenant now for nearly twenty years, never dreaming that I should be disturbed in any way! you now take away half the shooting and increase the rent, and that after I have spent 2000*l.* in building a good house on your land."

" Is that so, Peacock?" says the Duke.

"Yes, your grace, it is so."

" Then pay him for his house, and then we start fair," says the Duke.

SEASON 1873.

The accounts in the early spring were very cheering. On the 1st of April Black wrote to congratulate us on excellent prospects, not a bad bird had he seen since we left in September. There was a grand breeding stock, and he anticipated splendid shooting.

But it was not to be. On the 15th he writes reporting birds looking badly diseased, and on the 30th writes again that a third of the birds were dead.

It was sickening news, but there was hope yet, as a fair breeding stock was left, and the disease appeared to have spent itself, the birds nesting fairly well.

At the beginning of July disease again broke out, and with greater virulence, young and old birds falling before it; but David begged us to come, of course, in August and shoot down all we could, and so sweeten the ground for those that remained by stamping out all that was possible.

Disease prevailed over nearly all Scotland; amongst others, Glenmarkie was very bad. We did not put any birds on the table, and I sent none to my friends. What few good-looking birds there were went to London, and the scarcity through the country may be imagined when I say that they made 19*s*. a brace.

Bag.				Dalnawillan and Rumsdale
Grouse	...	...	...	...	151 brace.
Sundries	...	...	...	...	24 ,,

My chums were pretty miserable, and so was I.   It was a bitter disappointment.   No word from D. as to taking a gun for the next season, and in about a week or ten days they both went south.   However, I had to make the best of it, and, leaving my family at Dalnawillan, I went iuto Sutherlandshire trout fishing for a fortnight with my son Douglas, and after that we all went home.

Caithness, in those days, was the worst mapped county in Great Britain.   There was a good estate map of the Ulbster estates, and the maps were pretty reliable for a few miles from the coast.   Sutherland, belonging mainly to one proprietor, was well mapped.

On Dalnawillan we had a loch—a long walk across very bad ground from the lodge—that held, both in size and quality, the best trout in Sutherland and Caithness, but not plentiful; the best I ever did was eighteen fish in a day, but eight of them weighed $9\frac{1}{4}$lb., the largest being $1\frac{3}{4}$lb., and that was the largest size they ever reached, and, generally, a day's fishing meant eight or ten, with the half of them the larger size.   A predecessor of mine at Dalnawillan assured me that many were got up to 3lb. and 4lb.; it is marvellous the falsehoods men will commit themselves to as to size of fish—men perfectly reliable in other ways.

The gillies talked a good deal about a loch in Sutherland, not far off our march, where the fish were nearly as large and good, and very free to rise.   That sounded very nice, and needed to be experimented, and my son Douglas and I said we would take it on our way into Sutherlandshire.

In those days the lochs of Sutherlandshire were free to the angler, and for some years the Duke made it a condition in letting shootings that it should be so, and as the bulk of the lochs were difficult of access, and anglers few, there was no friction ; and in the summer months there were generally two or three rod men stopping at Auchentoul Inn, on the Helmsdale Strath.

In the old Scotch fashion, the inn was part inn and part shooting lodge, and in this case Sir John Karslake's keeper kept the inn, so everything was well regulated, and caused no annoyance to Sir John or his deer. Sir John was always courteous and pleasant.

Auchentoul Inn was twelve miles cross country— and very cross country—from Dalnawillan, and we sent our portmanteau to Dunbeath, sixteen miles, thence by coach, sixteen miles, to Helmsdale, and there to wait a chance lift up the Strath, eighteen miles, to Auchentoul.

We also ordered a machine from Auchentoul to meet us at Forsinean, ten miles by a decent road.

Willie Hunter, one of our gillies, vouchsafed to pilot; he had herded sheep at this Loch Sletil, and knew all about it. The ordnance maps now tell us that it is seven and a half miles from Dalnawillan, across a very bad piece of moorland and flow.

We left Dalnawillan at 8.30 a.m.—that is, David, Douglas, and I, and Hunter as pilot; a nasty, wet, drizzling rain ; encased in macintoshes, wet outside with rain and inside with perspiration, and after two and a half hours tramping and slushing over the wet moors, Willie pulled up, and in a very confused manner stated that we ought to be at the loch; " anyhow, it used to be here," said Willie.

A council was held to determine the present location

" Well ! I know the loch used to be just here."

of this wandering loch, and a deviation of half a mile to the right put us upon it.   Willie returned.

After a rest we donned wading stockings, and put rods together ; it would be 12 o'clock by the time we began ; we had some nice fish, largest 1lb., but our wading stockings would not put us into sufficiently deep water for the larger fish ; but we saw enough to convince us that the loch was not overstated.

We fished away, and packed up about 6 p.m. to make our way across the moor to Forsinean.

Again we missed our way ; we took the shoulder of Ben Sletil too high up, and it was getting dark when we struck the road, as it turned out, a mile on the Auchentoul side of Forsinean. Of course no machine.

It was raining; it had rained the whole day, and looked as if it meant to rain for a week, and we took off our macintoshes to lighten the walk—we could not get much wetter. Presently we met a shepherd, who told us Forsinean and the trap were behind us, and, telling him to send the trap after us, we tramped the hard road the whole nine miles, arriving at the same time as the trap that followed.

Our portmanteau did not arrive till next morning, but the innkeeper found us dry flannels and a good supper ; it was then 10 o'clock.

C. was very hopeful that grouse matters would quickly mend, and stuck to it for another season, and after that I was left with the whole cost of the affair for the following season, and seasons after that, which, with rent, keeper, and expenses, was not less than £700 a year, and nothing to shoot either, which was the worst part of the business.

E

SEASON 1874.

Neither C. nor I went near the place. Disease was gone, and so were the birds. It could have been truthfully advertised as perfectly free from disease, and lightly shot the previous season. In May, before nesting time, David hunted every beat, and found just fifty-two pairs of birds on the whole 24,000 acres.

In August he again hunted, and came across exactly the same number of broods as he had found pairs they certainly were grand broods, averaging eight to a brood, and he managed to kill out nearly all the old cock birds, leaving but one old bird to each brood.

Dunbar was very unhappy, and, of course, I was the same, and we arranged to have a consultation, and I met him in Edinburgh, where he had occasion to be. Dunbar summed up the whole thing by saying, in his plump way, there must be no birds whatever killed for two years at least.

Glutt, in some way, was, fortunately, off Dunbar's shoulders, and on the hands of the proprietor, who had it in hand for three years afterwards, when Dunbar took it off his hands at a moderate rent.

Strathmore was still on lease, the lease expiring after the season of 1874, and, backing his opinion that no birds should be killed in 1874, he arranged with the tenants that, in consideration of no grouse being taken off, he would abate half the year's rent.

He asked me if I would take Strathmore off his hands for the remaining fourteen years of his lease. "You shall have the whole 19,000 acres, including Achlybster, for £350 a year." But I was not a jobber in moors, and already had more than enough on my hands; but, if I had been clear of Dalnawillan, I think I would have closed with him.

The railway was making, and as the Rumsdale beats are too far away from Dalnawillan Lodge to shoot them conveniently from there, Dunbar suggested that I should build a small lodge near to the proposed station, and let off 10,000 acres of the Rumsdale side of Dalnawillan so soon as the stock of birds would warrant it.

That idea suited me down to the ground, as the remaining 13,000 or 14,000 acres attached to Dalnawillan was ample for the personal shooting of myself and sons, with, perhaps, a friend; the idea was eventually carried out at the proper time.

In July Douglas and I went to Rhiconich, on the west coast of Sutherland, for a fortnight's sea trout fishing. It was a disappointment; firstly, it was dry hot weather, that, of course, stopped sea trout fishing.

In the evening the midges were something unbearable, and drove us on to the sea loch trolling for lythe. We were pretty successful, but very soon used up everything in the shape of phantoms and spinners, and had to take to small trout for spinning.

So soon as a lythe of any size took your spinner, down he went into the seaweed tangle, and many were lost and the spinner with him.

.. We managed to get twenty-one lythe, weighing 83lb., of which some were up to 10lb., but we lost most of the best fish in the weeds.

On our way back we stopped at Overscaig, on Loch Shin, for a day's trout fishing, ending in a very fatiguing fiasco; we had a boat and two rowers, David and a gillie from the inn.

The morning was a nice fishing morning, and we made our way down to the Faig mouth, and got on pretty well, but, the wind changing, we put across to the other shore, and fished away.

As the day wore on, the wind increased, blowing a gale straight down the loch, so we got out of the boat, and, with a good deal of trouble, hugging the shore, the two men managed to get her back to just opposite Overscaig.

There we found two other men, who had come up from Lairg, and were in the same fix as ourselves.

It was raining heavily as well as blowing.

Taking advantage of a lull of wind, we tried to get across, but when a third way across, the wind again rose, and we had our work to do to edge the boat head to wind to gain the shore without an accident.

What was to be done? asked the other party. I said that I saw nothing for it but to walk round the head of the loch. They consulted with their boatman as to this, and then said they could not do it. Certainly, they had come out with thin boots and frock coats and white shirts, as they would have done on a fine afternoon at Richmond, totally unfit to face a wild Highland night,

"We have had no dinner," says one; "of course, we expected to get to Overscaig to dinner." "Well," I said, "we have a little of our lunch left, and you are welcome;" but they turned away. I believe they thought I was chaffing them.

However, there was the choice of stopping out on the moor that wild night or footing it, and we chose what we thought the lesser of two evils.

It was a very long three miles to head the loch and the swamp at the top. The shore of the loch was very deep peaty boggy ground, broken every fifty yards with deep gullies and burns and drains, clambering down and clambering up.

It was then quite dark, a howling wind and rain in our teeth.

At last, with nearly two hours' work, we crossed the Alt Na Ba Burn, and, heading the swamp, got to the river that connects Loch Graim with Loch Shin.

But, horror! the river was in spate, and not safe to cross.

We felt dead beat, and sat down in the wet; we had a little whiskey and water, but nobody said anything; one tried to light a pipe, but the matches were wet, and so was everything else outside our skins. We tried to look at our watches, but too dark to see them.

It was getting towards midnight. We started again, keeping along the banks of the river, to look for a ford. Near the outlet of Loch Graim the river was wider, and therefore the stream not so strong, and the bottom was hard. I had a long landing-net staff, and piloted the way; the water was up to the bottom of the waistcoat—an even depth, and gravel bottom, so we were all quickly safe across. Folks will say what a fuss about crossing up to your middle; yes, but handicap it with a dark howling night, an unknown ford, and all your courage already pretty nearly pumped out of you, and it will not be found to be quite so simple as it looks.

There was yet a mile of swampy walking over moorland, in the direction of the road, before it was struck, but then we were not more than two and a half miles from the inn, and soon put that behind us.

It was 1.30 a.m. when we reached the inn; they were waiting up most anxiously, fearing some serious accident, but could hardly credit that we had headed the loch, and on such a fearful night.

I have had many long wet moorland tramps, but nothing approaching to our Loch Shin episode.

I told David to see that our gillie had a good tea and eating, and some hot whiskey and water, but he came back to say the fellow was so thoroughly beat that he had gone to bed, too tired and done up to eat or drink anything.

SEASON 1875.

In June I went to Dalnawillan trout fishing.

The Thurso river rises in the heights of the Glutt shootings on the Sutherland march amongst a bewildering labyrinth of flows and black morasses, hideous, and gaunt. I have seen the inside of most Scotch wildernesses, but there is nothing anywhere within the four seas—aye, take in Ireland as well—that at all approaches the plateau from which descend the Berriedale, the Halladale, the Thurso, and the northern water shed of the Helmsdale, at a height of about 1400ft. above the sea.

The Thurso, commencing and for many miles a mere burn, descends from the heights through low flats, interspersed with three rocky gorges or glutts (from which, no doubt, the name of the shooting), of from half a mile to a mile each in length, the burn tumbling through them in a succession of small falls and rocky pools; and in the lowest gorge was a waterfall or force, as it would be termed in Yorkshire or Westmoreland.

One day fly fishing up the river, as far up as the entrance to the first gorge, I tried some of the rocky pools. They were quite unsuitable for the fly, but I took a number of pretty, little, bright trout.

Talking it over with the gillies next day, they said there was no remembrance of anybody ever having

taken any fish with rod and line, or any other way, up
in the rocky water.

Well, I bethought myself, as I felt sure there would
be fish as far up as there was water, and that something might be done with the worm worth talking
about in a small way.

I was an adept in that style of fishing, having had
much experience and success in fishing small wooded
brooks in Warwickshire. My mode of fishing was
with a three-jointed light stiff bamboo rod, bored
down the middle; the line, a very thin one, passing
through and out at a hole near where the hand holds
the bottom joint.

When too long take off the bottom joint; no reel,
simply a few yards of line running loose behind, the
hook whipped to one or two feet of gut, and one
No. 6 shot about six inches above the hook, having
no rings, no line bagging, you could push in the point
of the rod anywhere, and drop the worm by shaking
the rod.

A large bag of small worms was provided, and the
tackle Stewart fashion, but with two small hooks
only, and pretty fine gut.

Davia and I started away, and were at the foot of
the lower gorge by 10 a.m., David behind me; and
soon the fun was fast and furious, every little fall and
the pool below it, the worm no sooner in the bubbles
and froth than tug, tug, tug. " Lift him out, unhook
him David and bait again ; no, the worm will do." Tug
again; " Unhook him and bait this time." Tug again.
" Well, three out of that little hole is not so bad !"

David was disgusted at messing with such trash, as he termed it, but soon even he warmed to it.

The waterfall had a nice pool scooped out by the falling water, and, standing down stream below the fall, thirty came out of that place.

It was great fun to come across water and fish in these islands that were totally unsophisticated.

We worked up and up for miles, until the burn—aye, and the fish too—began to get very small, and at five o'clock we turned back, fishing a few of the best places on our way. The waterfall gave but two more, and I expect that was the last two in the pool.

Weighed at the lodge, deducting the basket, they scaled just 23½lb., and counted out 188 trout, just eight to the pound, and pretty little bright fellows they were.

David looked at them deprecatingly; repentance at being a party to anything so derogatory had come over him, and he viewed them philosophically, with the sole remark, "What a mess!"

My fishing was in low water. My son Douglas went up a few days after, meeting a rise of water, and he also had a great number, but out of places that I had not fished in low water.

The waterfall yielded none.

The burn was tried again on another day, but it was done for a season or two; as in other things in the world, you can't eat a cake and have it.

In August I took down my family party for their holidays. There would be little or nothing to shoot, a few cock birds to pick out of the broods and some

sundries, of course. The boys could fish away for
trout and get a few odd salmon out of the Upper
Thurso and Loch More, but they were very coppery
and red at that season.

During the first fortnight David and I hunted the
whole of the ground, killing the old cocks out of the
broods when opportunity occurred..

The increase of birds was very satisfactory, quite
150 broods on the ground, and fine broods too.

Bag.	Dalnawillan and Rumsdale.
Grouse	38½ brace.
Sundries	57½ brace.

Dunbar had been very fortunate, and let Strathmore
to an old connection ; rather more birds had been left
by the scourge on the lower beats of Strathmore than
on Dalnawillan. Those beats are the best ground
in Caithness, and if there are any birds there they
naturally will be. Dunbar looked the matter well in
the face, told the tale, the whole tale, and let it on a
seven years' lease, commencing, if I remember right,
with a rent of £300, increasing up to £575, or thereabouts.

The gentleman who took it knew exactly what he
was about. The good years that would accrue after
disease were before him.

The year after the expiration of the seven-year
lease and cycle, disease was again ravaging, and
there was little or no shooting for two or three years
after that.

The new tenant nursed the birds the first season,
killing only a few cocks or so.

In September, with one of the boys, I went over to Orkney, to try the fishing of the Loch of Stennes. We landed from the tub of a steamer that plied between Scrabster and Stromness, after a terribly bad passage across the Pentland Firth. The tide ran very strong, the wind met it, and the steamer, built on the lines of a walnut shell, rolled about in the trough of the sea.

We landed, and hiring a cart to carry our traps, tramped away to the top of the loch in Harray parish, and lodged with Peter Flett, farmer and miller.

The trout were most beautiful, equal to any sea trout, but not plentiful, anyhow very stiff to rise; they ran all sizes. Our best day to two rods was 17½lb., the largest scaling 2lb. 6oz.

On one other day we had fish of 1lb. 4oz. and 1lb., and amongst our take were some half-pound sea trout.

The loch was terribly ottered by the small farmers and crofters, but with very coarse horse-hair tackle. Certainly they did not get many; but, no doubt, that put them down from rising to the fly.

The ottering was not poaching, because every freeholder had the right, and nearly all were freeholders.

I asked Flett where he got his land from. "My father," said he; "and he had it from his father, and his father before him." I dare say if Peter and I could have traced it we should have found that the title commenced with his Scandinavian ancestors, who stole the land from the Pict, who lived in an underground house designed after the pattern of an improved fox-earth.

"What is done with the younger sons, Flett?"

"Oh, they go to the fishing, or into the Hudson Bay Co.'s employment." That was primogeniture with a vengeance. I wonder what the land reformers would have to say to that.

"Flett, what deeds have you to show?"—"Deeds! what do we want with deeds?"—"Well, suppose you want to mortgage."—"Orkney people don't mortgage," says Flett, with his nose in the air.

In a few days we had enough.

We loaded our traps on Peter's cart, and returned to Stromness, looking at an underground Pict's house on the way, where perhaps Flett's ancestor had disposed of the aborigines, by smoking them, and stopping up the outlets, as you would stifle rats.

Also we saw the Stones of Stennis, which, as Druidical remains, rank with Stonehenge.

We stopped on our way at the bridge that crosses the outlet of the loch to the sea, to try for sea trout. The tide water comes up to the bridge, and a little beyond, and from the bridge to the sea was about a mile.

On the rise and fall of the tide we landed six sea trout weighing 6½lb., the largest 2¾lb.

On the fall of the tide the sea trout stopped taking, and then the sillocks came as fast as possible. We had seventy-nine of them in little over an hour.

I was very much pleased with Orkney. The land was good, and the climate was better than that of the mainland.

There were some grouse, and, as far as I could

learn, the best moor was in Harray parish, where we had been fishing.

The moor was a common, and the whole of the commoners joined in granting a lease to the tenant of the shooting. I think the rent was £35 a-year, and he took off about 200 brace of grouse, and a really considerable number of snipe and plover, and I believe it was true that there was no disease. The game sold for more than paid the rent.

SEASON 1876.

Pretty much a repetition of the previous season; grouse were increasing fast, but none to spare for the gun.

I worked away at the cock birds, and let the boys get their hands in on the outside beats, where the birds would not be missed, breaking them in work as well as the dogs.

In the spring of this year, carrying out the idea propounded by Dunbar, utilising my experience of American house building in wood, of which I had taken careful particulars when in that country a year or two previously, I built a small lodge near to Altnabreac station, containing kitchen, parlour, and five bedrooms, and let it, with 12,000 acres of moorland, for three years—first year £200, second and third year at £300 a year, including keeper, with a proviso that if my keeper was of opinion that the birds could not be spared the bag should be limited to 100 brace in the first year, and in that event I was to return £100 of the rent.

I did limit them, and sent them a check for £100.

Bag.	Dalnawillan.	Rumsdale.
Grouse	112 brace ...	100 brace.
Sundries ...	54½ ,, ...	——

The railway was open and a station stuck down in

the middle of the moorland four miles from Dalnawillan Lodge and seven from Glutt, no road, or foot-
path even, in any direction from the station.

It was stuck down in the centre of the moorland to
take its chance.

For the use of Dalnawillan and Glutt Dunbar and I
did our best to induce the proprietor to make the four
miles of road that was needed.

We offered during the tenancy of our leases to pay
the proprietor six per cent. on the £600, which was
the estimated cost of the road, and do the repairs
ourselves, but of no avail. At last it was settled that
I should make the road and find the money, the cost,
with interest at five per cent., to be repaid to me by
twelve equal yearly instalments, of which the proprietor contributed half, Dunbar a quarter, and myself
a quarter. The road was made and open ready for
use for the shooting season of 1876.

After about a fortnight at Dalnawillan I took a trip
into Shetland with my boy Charlie, to verify the
wondrous tales of sea trout that were to be had in
every tidal stream and loch.

It was a miserable disappointment, every fish that
could be had was poached on the spawning beds and
by any other means at any other time; but on some of
the outer islands, I believe, matters were better.

What there were were very fine fish; we had nine
in all, four of which weighed 6½lb.

What a small world it is! Charley was fishing
away in Brouster Loch in waders up to his middle,

when someone calls out: " Holloa, Charley, what are you doing here?" And there was his class master at Clifton College also up to his middle.

· ' On our return to Caithness we had a horribly stormy passage from Lerwick to Wick, putting in for the night at Kirkwall in Orkney, to shelter from stress of weather.

Lerwick is a very pretty little town, the most northerly in Great Britain, doing a good and lively trade in fishing matters, and having a great many visitors in the season. For those cockneys who have the blessed faculty of defying *mal de mer*, and enjoying bottled porter and a pipe with the ocean in commotion— and my experience, so far as it goes, is that in those northern latitudes it always is in commotion—what can be a pleasanter or a cheaper sea trip than to go by the Aberdeen boat from London Bridge to Aberdeen, and thence to Lerwick *via* Wick, and round the islands in the trading steamer, and home by the West Coast.

Shetland from the outside looks very nice. It is indented in every direction with fiords, or voes they call them there, with very fine cliff scenery.

But the inside is dismal, the crofters and fishermen pare the turf and heather for winter bedding for their cattle, and, what with that and peat cutting for fuel, they leave the surface of the hills very black looking and hideous.

There is some good heather, perhaps about seven thousand acres, in the main island, and it would, no doubt, carry some grouse, if any means could be devised for destroying the swarms of greyback gulls, hoodie crows, and hawks.

Not a living thing can show, without being pounced upon and devoured. The only game of any description that I saw was two snipe ; not even a rabbit.

Before I went it had struck me as an anomaly that there should not be grouse, and I looked well into the question of whether grouse could be profitably introduced, but, looking at the small amount of moorland, and the large cost, if not impossibility of destroying the vermin, I gave up the notion. I notice from letters in the *Field* and elsewhere that others are agitating the question, and they will do well to thoroughly bottom the question before incurring heavy responsibilities.

One thing that strikes a visitor is the incessant knitting on the part of every woman and girl; no matter when or where, the knitting needles incessantly ply. Carrying baskets of peats from the hills in creels on their backs, still the needles ply in front.

Some of their knitting is very beautiful. The common goods are knitted from imported yarn, but the beautiful shawls are knitted from yarn spun from the fully-grown wool of the indigenous native sheep.

The wool is not clipped, but pulled when fully ripe.

The native sheep are of all colours, white, brown, yellow, &c., and many piebald.

With these colours the varied colours of the best quality Shetland shawls are derived from the natural colour of the wool, without dyeing.

F

Some of the shawls are exquisitely fine, and fetch large prices. For one, many yards square, I gave £5. Of course it was a unique specimen, and afterwards, in England, I was assured that it was a cheap purchase. It could be doubled up not much larger than a pocket handkerchief.

SEASON 1877.

At last a gleam of sunshine. Seasons 1873, '74, '75, and '76, four long years practically blank, and heavy expenses running the while; it was a heart-breaking business, worse than my experience in Banffshire. But at last I was to expect some moderate shooting for two guns, and my expectations were realised.

Bag.		Dalnawillan.		Rumsdale.
Grouse...	...	426½ brace	...	300 brace.
Sundries	...	85½ ,,	...	—

SEASON 1878.

This was to be really good shooting for two guns.

My son Oliver was to be home from New York for a holiday, and I reserved the shooting for him and myself, and very pleasant shooting we had. We shot together—

Bag.		Dalnawillan.		Rumsdale.
Grouse...	...	627½ brace	...	480 brace.
Sundries	...	64½ ,,	...	—

SEASON 1879.

This was the eighth year that I had paid rental for this moor, and this was the second year out of the eight that it would afford shooting for more than two guns.

I had a very fine stock of birds upon the ground. I had nursed the stock judiciously. I had not shot it down when recovering from disease, and at last the moor was full of birds, and for the next two or three years, until the scourge paid its next visit, we might shoot and hammer away at the birds, without detriment. Nothing that we could do in the way of shooting could possibly reduce the breeding stock below what it should be, until disease again reduced it.

I had relet the Rumsdale side, with 10,500 acres, for three years, at £300 per annum, leaving, say 13,500 acres to Dalnawillan shooting.

We laid ourselves out for a fine bag, and we had it.

I said to David, "Last season, shooting with Mr. Oliver, we made together over six hundred brace. Now, we have treble the birds we had to begin that season. If I go to work shooting steadily by myself, say seven hours a day for four days a week, can I take off 600 brace to my own gun and for once make a swagger bag?"—"Yes, you can," says David.—"Then I will do it," responded I; so it was arranged to shoot the ·moor in two parties, myself one party, and two guns in the other party; each party taking the beats fairly in turn.

The second party of two guns was made up of the three elder boys and a friend, shooting five days a week, weather permitting, taking their turns alternately, the men out, going after snipe and ducks and fishing.·

I started with 42 brace on the 12th, and on the 14th 52½ brace, and continued to make good bags. · On August 26, my fifty-eighth birthday, I came in with 50½ brace; it was the second time over the beat, and on September 15, in twenty-one days shooting, I numbered 617 brace, close upon an average of 30 brace a day besides sundries.

· Generally through Scotland moors had not fairly recovered their full complement of birds, and I believe it was acknowledged that 617 brace.was the best bag in Scotland made that season to one gun in the first five weeks shooting over dogs.

. We had a fine time and a very enjoyable time, and up to the 16th of September, when we went south, we had taken off 1138 brace.

In October I returned with two other men ·to shoot under the kite, and we took off just 200 brace. When at Glenmarkie, I could do nothing with the kite, the birds. rolled up before it and away for a couple of miles.

October shooting in Caithness and Sutherland over dogs under the kite when birds are plentiful, is very grand sport.   It is the acme of point shooting.·   ·· ·

In October the air is crisp and bracing, there is plenty of walking, and you are in the best condition, or you ought to be.

The kite is a large kite, much larger than the partridge kite used in England, and is flown very high, and so covers a large extent of ground. It is worked down wind in front of the gun, so the dog has to work down wind and on ticklish birds ; therefore I need not say that it requires clever old experienced dogs. Many good August dogs cannot get into it.

Packs of six to twelve birds rarely sit well; they rise at sixty to one hundred yards, but the small lots and single birds sit fairly well, rising at twenty to thirty yards.

They rise in front like a wisp of lightning, hardly well up before they turn to the right or left and away behind you. They should be taken just on the turn. It is very difficult to get in a second barrel unless, as they turn and go past they are near enough for a skimming side shot.

Good driving shots have said to me that the man who can walk and kill October grouse under the kite, and kill them well, can kill anything.

October sport with the kite is very uncertain. There may be too much wind or too little, and in that month you sometimes get very bad weather and more snow than is pleasant, and then of course birds are very wild and unsettled.

Big bags cannot be made under the kite; an

average of 15 brace per day to a gun is very good. I never managed to make 20 brace; twice I have made 19½, and could generally average 15.

There is an impression that the kite puts birds off the ground, and generally makes them wild; but I don't think so. Of course the beats are changed, and my impression is that it has no more effect than an eagle hovering and then going on.

Those who have kited and driven, tell me that driving disturbs and unsettles the birds far more than the kite.

Bag.	Dalnawillan.	Rumsdale.
Grouse ...	1338 brace. ...	900 brace.
Sundries ...	155½ ,, ...	—

A number of grouse were, in addition, killed by the keeper during the winter months.

The total to my own bag was 674 brace of grouse, and 48½ brace of sundries.

Season 1880.

Another grand season, the best out of the seventeen years of the lease.

On the first and second days I shot by myself, taking off fifty-four and forty-four and a half brace respectively. I was in very good form, and began by getting sixteen brace without slipping a cartridge.

After the first two days we shot in two parties of two guns each. Up to September 16, when we went south, we had 1284½ brace.

In October I returned, with another man, to shoot under the kite, and we made 188½ brace.

Bag.	Dalnawillan.	Rumsdale.
Grouse ...	1473 brace ...	1600 brace.
Sundries ...	128½ ,, ...	—

The sundries included ninety-seven snipe, the greatest number ever made in one season.

The Rumsdale party shot very hard almost every day to end of season.

A number of grouse were in addition killed by my keeper during the winter.

SEASON 1881.

Grouse had culminated to their highest level, the highest ever known in the record of the Dalnawillan moors, and were now to recede, and again undergo the scourge.

In the spring, birds were looking well, and in great plenty.

We could not say that there was disease amongst them, in fact, we could have conscientiously said that we had not seen a diseased bird. But, later on, we saw barren birds, nests not so well filled as they should be; and in August, many birds shabbily feathered on the legs, and thin breasted.

There was nothing like the quantity of birds as in the previous August, bad nesting would account for that. Some broods would, perhaps, jump up, with one or two miserable chirpers in addition to one old bird, and barren birds also were plentiful.

The moor was shot in two parties of two guns each, and afforded fair sport.

Bag.	Dalnawillan.	Rumsdale.
Grouse	822 brace ...	900 brace.
Sundries ...	73½ „ ...	—

We did not return in October, as the prospects were not sufficiently encouraging.

Season 1882.

I was anxious about the birds, in fact, in my own mind it was a foregone conclusion. But Black wrote in the spring to say that there was a fair stock upon the ground, and looking pretty well, though now and again seeing a bad bird, and he was inclined to think that disease was to pass over with the brush of the previous year; but disease was due, and I had my misgivings that history would repeat itself.

Nothing very particular occurred during the nesting season, and in August we went down, expecting some fair shooting, but it was not so; it was a great disappointment. With all our experience and careful watching of the state of the birds, they had died off—imperceptibly dwindled away since the spring.

Disease in this attack was very different in its aspect from former attacks. They come on very suddenly, sharp and decisive; but on this occasion I have no doubt but that it had been hanging about all through 1881, and also in the spring and summer of 1882, steadily wearing away the birds bit by bit.

There was little to shoot, and I agreed with my neighbours that we should all spare our birds, and nurse what were left. My tenant at Rumsdale would not hold his hand, and shot away, to my serious detriment, as it was the last year of his lease.

Bag.	Dalnawillan.	Rumsdale.
Grouse... ...	186 brace ...	300 brace.
Sundries ...	94 ,, ...	—

Season 1883.

Disease had worn itself through in the season of 1882, and birds were clean, but very scarce, in the spring of 1883, and needed careful nursing, so I went down for a few days, hunting the ground, and found a sprinkling of birds on Dalnawillan, and next to none on Rumsdale.

I killed all the cocks I could, and Black followed them up after I left.

Bag.			Dalnawillan.			Rumsdale.
Grouse	...	...	53 brace.	...	...	—
Sundries	...	...	54 brace.	...	...	—

SEASON 1884.

Dalnawillan, carefully considering the matter, could spare a few birds ; what breeding stock there was has done well, but there were not enough birds to make it worth while to take down a party, so I let the place for the season to two gentlemen, with a limit of 300 brace, of course, at a small rent.

The attraction was the fishing and a pleasant lodge and surroundings for their holiday.

By myself I went down for a fortnight to shoot on the Rumsdale ground, to take off just what I thought could be spared.

I found pretty well of birds on the beats adjoining Dalnawillan, and took off 170½ brace.

A fair, but moderate, breeding stock was left on both moors.

Bag.		Dalnawillan.		Rumsdale.
Grouse ...	...	300 brace.	...	170½ brace.
Sundries	...	97½ brace.	...	16 brace.

SEASON 1885.

Very pleasant shooting, bags not large, but enough to keep going ; game good and healthy.

I let Rumsdale to a gentleman, who shot by himself his own gun only.

Bag.	Dalnawillan.	Rumsdale.
Grouse	...	635½ brace.	...	439 brace.
Sundries	...	94 brace.	...	—

SEASON 1886.

A very good season, both on Dalnawillan and Rumsdale. Shooting up to Sept. 13th in two parties; of two guns each gave 1006½ brace, and in October a further bag of 205 brace to three guns; a most charming fortnight's shooting.

Bag.	Dalnawillan.	Rumsdale.
Grouse ...	1211½ brace. ...	673 brace.
Sundries ...	88 brace. ...	—

This season was to me a red letter year in Scotch sport; very considerable success rewarded my personal endeavours in every way.

During the month of April I fished on the Thurso and on Loch More, as one of the party of eight rods, all fishing from Strathmore Lodge, and I killed fifty-three salmon.

Sixteen of them, weighing 164½lb., I made in the one day, the 15th, to my own rod on No. 8 beat of the river. On that day good fortune seemed to attend me at all points; they were taking surely in heavy dead water pools, and I bagged every fish into which I bent the rod—a most unusual circumstance. Many never showed a rise, they sucked the fly under water.

The first fish damaged the fly, the next fourteen were taken with one fly, a small silver-grey, no change of fly, but retied several times to the single gut cast.

The last fish, a fifteen-pounder, I had moved in the morning, in fact the first rise, and the last thing before leaving off I crossed the river and changed for a larger size silver-grey as the light was failing, and at that he came like a lion.

Not a single hitch or contretemps occurred during the day. Certainly both myself and my gillie, Johnny Sinclair, were desperately careful, examining and proving knots of the gut casting line after every fish. We were in for a good thing, and nothing that care and attention would do was neglected.

That was the best day ever made on a Thurso river beat and still holds the record, and in all probability will continue to do so.

It was a very hard day's work; as the fish meant it, I meant it, and I kept the fly going without intermission, with an interval of ten minutes for lunch, from 9.30 a.m. to 7 p.m.

The next day, a Saturday, and also the Sunday, I laid up in the lodge with lumbago.

My good fortune still pursued me. My last fish at the end of the month was upon Loch More, and was the heaviest fish of the season, viz., 29lb., a magnificent clean run fish, and he was taken on the same silver grey that had killed fourteen fish on the great day. That fly killed twenty-three fish in the month, and is now assigned an honorary post in the fly box.

At the end of June, having obtained the necessary

permission from the higher powers, I fished the Baden lochs in Sutherlandshire for trout with the fly.

The lochs are three in number, and communicate, all on one level, by two short water ways, and, collectively, they cover some miles of ground.

Except to one shooting lodge they are nearly inaccessible, and the boats upon the lochs, belonging to the lodges, even if they had been available to me, were too large, needing two gillies to row them, and for trout fishing a large boat is a great drawback; you can't go to work too quietly, or too gently either, in boats or tackle. The shepherds' boat was light enough, but unsafe.

It is a notion that Sutherlandshire lochs need a large gaudy fly, but year by year I have been reducing the size of flies, and fining down the gut.

Again, what is called a fishing breeze is a mistake: if it comes, of course you must make the best of it; but to kill trout cleverly and quickly let me have fine tackle, a light 10ft. rod, and just a ruffle on the water, and if rain is falling and dimpling the water, the less wind the better; of course, if you fish big gaudy flies and double handed rods, you get little without a breeze.

To solve matters, I arranged to lodge with a shepherd not far from the side of the top loch; he gave me a room, and made me pretty comfortable, and with tea and whisky, good red fleshed trout, eggs, and a ham to cut at, I got along pretty well. Anyhow, I was on the ground, and close to my work, which was the main thing if I meant business.

G

I sent my own boat and gillie by rail, and then carted it over, so I had the right boat for the work, and a safe boat too, which is a point I always look to, as the squalls of wind get up very suddenly on those large lochs amongst the mountains.

I fished with great success, commencing June 30, and fished for seven consecutive days, Sunday, of course, excepted.

My total bag was 534 trout, weighing 198½lb., which is an average of over 28lb. per day; my best day was 113 fish, weighing 42½lb.

I have not come across any trout fishing scores that will beat this record of seven days fishing.

Fortune had again favoured me, excepting one day, when it was a blazing sun; they were all good fishing weather.

When August came, to my own gun my bag of grouse was five hundred and a half brace.

Of all sport I know nothing so deeply exciting as the steady head and tail rise of a heavy salmon, say a 20lb. fish, and the firm tug that you feel as he goes down.

Remember what Major Treherne says, " Don't strike, that tug has fastened the hook if it is to fasten;" but there is nothing so quietly satisfying as the feel on your hip of a heavy pannier of brown trout.

About the salmon you do as your gillie tells you, plant your foot on that rock, or on that sod, and cast there, and the fish comes (when he does come), as the fly swings round two yards below, or rather comes when he does come, the coming being a long way the exception; but the basket of brown trout has been your own doing—you have cast your little flies yard by yard where your own experience tells you the brown trout will come, and the gay little chap does come.

It is all your own act and deed: the gillie has had no hand in it, except bewailing the loss of time after those messing trout, when elsewhere there might be "just a chance" of the salmon that don't come.

I take it that it is every bit as sportsmanslike in its way to kill the little brown snipe, or the little brown trout, as to stalk the monarch of the glen, or rise the monarch of the stream. As regards the snipe, he is good to eat, and the monarch of the glen certainly not. I suppose for punishment of my sins, I once had to live for a week on the latter.

In passing, I may remark as to size of Scotch trout taken with the fly.

In my twenty-six years experience of Scotch fly fishing I have been accessory to the taking of only four fish exceeding 2lb. each in weight.

It is my experience that, excepting two or three lochs in Caithness and Sutherland, that the few fish that exceed 1lb., so soon as they attain that weight become predatory, feeding on their own species, that flies and insects will not maintain fish of that size in condition.

—ooᴑoo—

SEASON 1887.

Circumstances prevented my family going down (my boys were scattered in professional pursuits), so I determined to let Dalnawillan for August and September, and shoot at Rumsdale as a bachelor, and with two other men.

The weather turned out very disappointing and unsettled—daily storm showers; so consequently the results on both moors did not come up to my expectations.

In Rumsdale (why, I don't know) the weather was worse than in any other part of Caithness.

Only one day was I out without being interfered with by rainstorms.

In Dalnawillan the weather was rather better, and in Strathmore heavy and dull, but not much amiss.

In October, I went down to Dalnawillan with two other guns. There bad weather again followed us, but we managed to make 177 brace.

Bag.	Dalnawillan.	Rumsdale.
Grouse... ...	1223 brace. ...	561 brace.
Sundries ...	— ...	24 ,,

This season was the culminating season of that cycle, and we ought to have had better bags, but wet weather makes the birds wild and skittish. I had expected 1200 brace on Dalnawillan, and 800 on Rumsdale, as a minimum; the birds were there to do it.

SEASON 1888.

All things come to an end, and the seventeen years lease was drawing to a close.

This would be my last season, and I shot at Dalnawillan with two of my sons and a friend.

My family did not go down.

Unfortunately I was very lame with rheumatism in one leg, and could only get about a few hours every other day, puddling over the near beats and working the dogs myself, with a boy to lead a spare dog, and a gillie to carry the birds.

The other party were out every day, weather permitting, two guns to the party, and taking turn and turn about.

Disease was now again getting due. We had some indication the previous season, and this season we had them all over the moor—barren birds, small broods, a bad bird now and again; in fact, a repetition identical with the commencement of the attack of 1881, and about the same result as to bag, which, however, gave a fair amount of shooting.

On moors south and east there was little or no shooting; but Strathmore on the north was much better.

Bag.	Dalnawillan.	Rumsdale.
Grouse ...	816½ brace. ...	500½ brace
Sundries ...	61 ,, ...	—

On the 13th I went over to Thurso to say good bye to old friends, and the next morning I was away south, thus terminating my grouse shooting days and my long and pleasant connection with Caithness and its people, and the wild moorlands of Dal-a-vhuilinn or the Miller's Dale.

A HARE DAY.

The blue, or alpine hare, is, as all Scotch sportsmen know, a great nuisance in grouse shooting over dogs.

Do what you will there is in every dog an innate longing to chase or point ground game in preference to birds, and if blue hares are shot upon the grouse moor in the sight of the dogs, nothing that you can do will prevent the dog from pointing or drawing on the track of other hares.

On well regulated moors blue hares are looked upon as vermin, and all possible are killed in the late winter months, when they are white, by the keeper, and sent to market; but they make very small prices, not more than 9*d.* to a 1*s.* after paying carriage.

When at Dalnawillan in October, before leaving it was the rule to have a hare driving day on Ben Alasky with two or three guns, the result being generally about ninety hares and a few brace of grouse, and the number killed have been included in the record of sundries.

All the gillies, boys, shepherds, &c., were on that occasion pressed into the service.

There were two hills adjoining one to the other, Ben Alasky and Glass Kerry, both about 1100ft. high, and both were driven.

The party started about 11 a.m. from the lodge, beaters and guns forming a line, taking the ground before them to about half way up Glass Kerry, getting on the way two or three hares and a brace or two of grouse.

Then the guns were sent forward to their posts.

The line of beaters sweep round the hill.

Perhaps fifteen to twenty hares may be had. Luncheon is then taken on the ridge connecting the two hills.

After luncheon the beaters in line start well at the bottom of Ben Alasky, gradually beating round and round in a spiral until they reach the summit.

It may take two hours.

It is the habit of the blue hare to mount the hill, but some few break back.

The guns are in three butts, the first butt on the summit of the hill, and the other two on the slope below.

Odd grouse skim over the butts and fall to a clever shot.

At times the hares come up in considerable numbers, and the single gun (no loader) gets hot; but if a hare escapes the one butt it gets across the fire of another butt, and so very little escapes.

Then comes the collection of the slain and crippled, and loading men and gillies with the slain.

The reader may say, Why not send a cart or pannier pony? simply because the peat moss of Caithness is too soft to carry a pony.

It was a pleasing little shoot, and the weather at that time of year being generally stormy, the outlook from the hill was very grand.

REMARKS ON THE OUTCOME OF DISEASE.

A perusal of the foregoing reminiscences will show that grouse shooting, like other sports, is very uncertain, and that really good shooting cannot apparently be looked for in more than four seasons out of seven, consequent on the ravages of disease.

With the exception of portions of Southern Perthshire say the district west of Dunkeld, embracing the Breadalbane Moors, which for many years have had comparative immunity from disease, but will have it sooner or later, the moors of Aberdeen, Banff, Inverness, Ross, Sutherland, and Caithness are attacked at pretty regular intervals, and an old and experienced hand may spot the years of disease pretty well in advance.

In Sutherlandshire the recovery is rather slower than in Caithness, and the period of good shooting rather less.

On the smaller moors on the north-east of Caithness mixed up with the arable land there is certainly very much less disease, and when the birds get a touch, it is called a bad breeding season ; as the tenant of a very fair moor in that district put it, " We never have disease, but we had a season of poor shooting as the birds did not breed that year." Of course, that meant disease.

I take it that in that district, the climate being better, the ground carrying few birds and being sprinkled in patches mixed with arable, that the risk of contagion is less, besides which, from the tendency of birds to draw down from the higher to the lower grounds in the storms of winter, the gaps caused by disease get filled up.

The same remarks will apply to Orkney, and, more favourably still, excepting that they do not fill up from the higher ground; but in Orkney the moors are very small, and no great quantity of grouse.

Are we to draw our conclusion from the experience of previous years, not of one cycle, but of several.

If we are to avail ourselves of past experience, the inference derived is that disease does run in cycles, and that it is a provision of Providence to ensure the survival of the fittest, and thus prevent the gradual decadence of the grouse.

It would appear that grouse shooting runs in years pretty much thus:

1st year.—Say disease; shoot down and stamp out as far as possible.

2nd year.—A jubilee; but shoot old cocks.

3rd year.—A jubilee; but shoot old cocks.

4th year.—Moderate shooting; be careful not to overdo it to the serious detriment of the good years before you.

5th year.—⎫ Grand shooting. Shoot down all
6th year.—⎬ you can, and so get off all you can
7th year.—⎭ before disease does it for you.

But if the moor be shot ever so lightly in the second

and third years it is simply killing the goose for the golden egg, your moor will not recover its stock and give good shooting until the seventh year or the eve of the next cycle.

The laird will say, " Eh! I shall get breeding stock from my neighbours ;" but what if his neighbours are at the same foolish game.

My own experience has been not to let a moor, excepting on lease, until I am quite certain that it can properly afford the number of birds to which I may limit it, and I think that I have pretty clearly shown that it will not afford birds at all in the first and second years, perhaps a few in the third, the killing of old cocks excepted, which should be done by the keeper.

The present modern practice of letting moors from year to year, quite irrespective of whether from the ravages of disease there are grouse to afford shooting, and so leading to the destruction of the little breeding stock that may exist, has ruined and destroyed the reputation of many fine moors that will carry heavy stocks of birds if properly treated.

They year after year yield little or no sport, and naturally get a bad repute until they are again caught by disease and shelved for further years.

The laird has to make up his mind to one of two options :

1. To let his moor on lease at a low reasonable rent ; or

2. To retain his moorland, and nurse the birds until

the moor is full, and then let at a higher rent either for one year or more.

Any other course is suicidal to him in the long run ; he may deceive his client, and perhaps himself, and get a heavy rent for one year and then he is done.

In the season of 1883, with a full knowledge that the moor has been cleaned out with disease and over shooting in 1882, I was asked, will you let me Rumsdale with a limit of 150 brace for £100.

My reply was, that firstly there was not 150 brace upon the moor, and that if I let it I should be cheating him, and that if I did, shooting the little there was would do me far more damage by the loss of the breeding stock than the value of the £100, or three or four times the £100.

It is difficult to educate people to the knowledge of the fact that the breeding of grouse is like the breeding of other animals or birds, and that grouse are not in some mysterious way showered down by Providence like manna in the desert.

It is appreciated as regards pheasants, but appears that it has yet to be learned as regard grouse.

I have remarked that as a rule moors are more readily let, and higher rents are obtained in the disease year, the year following the cycle of three or four big years, than at any other period.

Men are jubilant and excited over the successes of the three or four previous years, the prestige and the glamour are fostered by those in the interest of letting, and folks are unwilling to believe, as I was in the season of 1866, that such magnificent sport can collapse almost at once to nothing.

Disappointments result for a couple of years or more, and then moors become very unsavoury, and really good places are on hand, and at moderate rents for the ensuing three or four years.

It is evident that if history is to repeat itself, that, looking at the cost of keeper and other expenses, it is cheaper to rent for three or four years at a high rent than to take for seven years at a low rent, taking your chance, or, more properly speaking, the certainty, of the fat and the lean.

Anyone about to take a moor of fair repute may, by taking the necessary trouble before he signs the agent's agreement to pay £500 or £1000 for what Providence may send him, ensure himself the sport represented by the high rent.

According to the amenities of the place—for the number of brace to be killed is not the only factor in fixing the price—the rent will vary from 10s. to 20s. a brace, and an intending tenant should not grudge it if he gets the sport.

Let the moor be run with dogs by a competent keeper, and he will tell you if there is sufficient breeding stock to breed the promised 1000 brace.

Then ascertain, *positively and absolutely*, when the last attack of disease occurred; it will be the year after the last successful season.

Then take the moor for a term of years, ending in the seventh year from the date of the disease year.

Those moors that suffer the most in their disease

year, like the moor in Strathspey, referred to in Season 1871, will probably afford the heaviest shooting in their good years.

Grouse, of course, have other drawbacks besides disease.

If the moors are on high ground, they are liable to have eggs frosted in late frosts, or young grouse killed by late snowstorms, as occurred in Season 1864 on Glenshee. Again, you may have a lazy, whiskey drinking keeper, who neglects verminkilling; but, as a rule, once out of the egg, the young bird is safe.

HEATHER BURNING AND DRAINING.

Indiscriminate burning of heather is another great drawback on Sutherland and Caithness moors.

In Caithness, it will take fourteen or more years to grow deep, good heather on the hill moors, and in Sutherland eight or ten.

The upper moors of Caithness, and also of parts of Sutherland, carry very little really good heather; in fact, only on the burn banks or dry knolls does it grow.

The remainder of the ground is broken, knotty peat bog, with short stunty heather, and stretches of deer grass, with wet flows on the upper flats. All good shooting ground in fine weather, and birds like it then.

Birds rely on the deep heather for shelter and food in the winter. Burn that out, and they go where they can find it, and don't return. It is just the same as if you burn down a crofter's house and his crops, he must move on to somewhere else.

Some of the best moors in Caithness have been ruined, and cannot be recovered for very many years, to the very serious loss of the proprietors, from incessant burning and shooting down breeding stock after disease, both attributable to the almost culpable negligence, certainly ignorance, of those in charge of the regulation of the burning and the letting of the moors.

The burning is a far more serious business than the shooting down of stock.

One fool of a factor did say to me (he is dead and gone, or I would not name it), "Perish every grouse, before a blade of grass shall suffer."

The sheep rent on the moor to which the above referred is gone because sheep do not now pay on that ground, and the grouse rent—the best rent of the two—is also gone, because the heather is burned off clean as the back of your hand.

In Dalnawillan, heather burning has been with me a constant wrangle with the proprietor or his representatives, or the sheep farmers, no matter the clear agreements to the contrary, protecting the heather. If I was fighting anybody's battle, it was in the interest of the proprietor; the question was one far more important to him than to me.

. Burning, to do it properly, is a very expensive process on such extensive ranges as the Caithness moors.

In Dalnawillan and Rumsdale, it needed four parties during the early part of April, to do it properly, four men in each party. One man to kindle, and keep on kindling; the other three men armed with birch brooms, watching and regulating the course of the fire, beating it out where it unduly spreads, or beating it out altogether to rekindle in case of a change of wind in a wrong direction.

Unless the weather is quite dry for a week or more, the rough ground and deer grass, both of which it is most desirable to burn in the interest of grouse and sheep, will not burn, and when your staff of men are collected and got together, a sudden storm of rain or snow comes on, and you are delayed for a week, and perhaps put off altogether for that season.

Naturally, if you are prevented by weather from burning, the sheep farmer is annoyed, because he does not get his burning done. He argues, " Let me burn; I will burn as much in a day as you will in a week." And so he would, but it would be the fine old heather that will burn, and the shooting value of the moor destroyed for many long years.

I do not say that sheep farmers or their shepherds desire to burn, and damage the shooting tenant, and also the proprietor (not that the latter or his factor understand the question or appreciate the damage) by burning out patches of good heather, the burning of which destroys the cover appertaining to hundreds of acres, and so destroys the shooting.

One shepherd certainly, said he liked the ground burned, because it was easier walking.

But if the shepherd is to burn, what can he do by himself.

He can do no more than kindle a fire, and let the winds of heaven take it how and where it likes.

To get a good fire, he will get his back to the wind, and kindle a well-heathered burn, and make a good clear sweep for half-a-mile, and so destroy the shelter of five or six hundred or more acres for a dozen years or more.

I have seen two miles in a blaze at one time, but not on my ground ; it was too well looked after.

H

SURFACE DRAINING.

I am convinced that much may be done in improving grouse ground in the north of Scotland. Make ground habitable and suitable for grouse, and they will come without any further trouble.

Grouse like wettish ground, especially in hot weather, presuming that there is dry ground available for them to nest upon, and feed and sit upon in wet weather.

Now, by judicious surface draining, much may be done.

When the ground slopes from the low hills, the surface water works over the face of the ground, thoroughly soddening it, and rotting the heather that would otherwise grow.

The drains are simply small sheep drains cut on the surface, slantingly across the slope, wherever there is fall enough just to run the water.

The drain intercepts the water, runs it off, preventing it from running over the ground below the drain, and immediately dries the ground immediately *below the drain*. Heather grows some yards wide, and there the birds will sit and nest, and you have created increased grouse ground.

The expense, in view of the benefit is very trifling. A pair of drainers during the summer months, say a cost of £50, will get over a very large extent of ground.

The proprietor was constantly endeavouring to sell the property, in which event my lease would drop through, and he was impervious to any arrangements as to draining, otherwise I should have done the whole of the Dalnawillan ground. As it was, I did do some odd bits, at my own cost. One beat, near the lodge, I scored over with a few hundred yards of draining, and converted it from a bad to a good beat.

Such draining, of course, improves the ground for sheep as well as grouse.

I presume the time will come when proprietors will see that profit will accrue from cultivating their moors for the purpose of carrying grouse, by endeavouring in all ways to improve the heather by judicious burning and draining, in sufficient amounts to carry as large a stock as is reasonable for the extent of ground. I see no reason whatever, if you offer as favourable conditions to the birds, why they should not be as plentiful on ground A as on ground B; as a matter of fact they will be.

DOGS.

To some men (certainly it is so to me) one great element of the pleasure of walking shooting *versus* standing shooting, viz., the driving of grouse, partridge, and pheasant, is the working and use of dogs where they are useful and essential to success, in the particular sport for which they are used.

Do not let it be inferred that I am detracting from driving, or the skill and experience that is necessary to do it well, both in beaters and guns.

Each sport is delightful in its way and in its season.

The Yorkshire grouse cannot be brought to bag without driving, and so with partridges and pheasants in certain counties.

But I do feel more delight in hunting the game than in having the game hunted towards me.

I have always worked a perfect retriever broken by myself and kept to myself, a dog keen to his work, and who keeps by your side, not at heel, as he needs to see what is doing, if he is to help you to his uttermost, who keeps his nose on the alert, and tells you by a look when you are passing a close sitting partridge or rabbit or hare in its form, and who tells you if the partridge covey is still in front or run up the right or left furrows of the swedes, who stops with you until told to go, and then goes quietly back to where he saw the bird drop, and takes up the scent of the dead or running bird ; not a dog who, when told to go rushes and tears about hoping to flush the winged bird into sight, or put up and chase some wretched rabbit, which is far more to his taste.

I have never done any good with pedigree dog-blood as shown on the show bench. Of course, on the show bench it is not pretended for one moment that any good is to accrue in a sporting sense; all is sacrificed to shape, size, and coat, which in a sporting dog get it if you can, but probably you have to do without some points if you get brains and keenness.

Napoleon, Wellington, and Gen. Sheridan were all small men, and their physique would not have commanded prizes on the show bench.

Again, for field trials dogs are bred up for that business only, and are rarely used for sporting.

At a field trial you want a bold pretentious dog that will go in and do just one or two things in a certain form, stand hares and rabbits, if he does it in proper form, and as to whether he is an industrious good worker, that is a matter of indifference. A really good dog, if a little shied by the crowd round him, will be quite out of the running in a field trial. I don't say but that some field trial dogs may possess high qualities that are useful as a cross in breeding.

I raise no objection to dog shows, they afford pleasure to numbers of people. What I desire is that the inexperienced sportsman shall not look in that direction for his sporting dogs.

Caithness birds, especially in catchy weather, run very much when pointed and drawn upon. Clearly, like a red-leg partridge, he tries his legs well before he will take to wing. . Sometimes they will road over 100 yards or more, and it is an unexplained mystery to me how a brood will cross a burnt and bare patch in front of you as fast as you can comfortably walk, without showing themselves.

Old solitary cocks are terrible fellows for this, and if your dog does not foot them fast they will outwalk you, and ultimately rise wild.

One old brute pointed well fifty yards within the march, took me such a distance across the Dunbeath march that I began to be so thoroughly ashamed of my trespass, that when he did rise and drop to the shot, I felt half inclined to let him lie and come away.

To my mind working a brace of dogs is a mistake.

Rap, we will say, gets birds and Ben backs him; certainly a very pretty picture, if the dogs do it well.

The birds draw on, and Rap draws on, Ben remains behind, stands like a fool—the poetry of the picture is gone, perhaps he draws on in Rap's footsteps.

Besides if you want to work your dogs in pairs you will need double the number in the kennel, ay, and an extra dog breaker as well.

In the course of a six or seven hour day, to work a party, you will need, if you work them singly, three experienced dogs and two younger ones coming on to work.

In Caithness and Sutherland necessarily wide ranging a little over two hours early in the season, is enough for an old dog, and less for a young one coming on, and four days a week is about as much as they will do, and if the gun shoots four days a week, it is as much as he can do to shoot properly. A man who is careful of himself will get more birds in four easy days, than the enthusiast who works long hours and six days.

If you want to get birds, keep yourself and dogs and gillies fresh and in good form, and so that when birds rise they shall also fall.

I have heard of dogs that will work all day long and every day as well, but I have never yet been fortunate enough to come across that very remarkable and desirable strain.

Here let me give a sketch that is no mere flight of fancy.

The 26th of August, my birthday.

It is a sunny day with a gentle balmy wind, and the heather, which is full in bloom, is dusting your boots white with its pollen.

It is a lazy day for birds, and they will not much care to run.

Daisy is ranging pretty wide, and, getting an indication of birds, pulls up and looks over her shoulder towards her master.

"Has she birds, David?" "She is no sure." You walk slowly up to Daisy, she draws on, and her point gradually stiffens; another twenty yards and she stops full point; you both walk on, the old cock bird rises first at twenty-five yards, and he goes down, you load, and the hen and three young birds rise within ten yards.

Take it calmly, don't smash up the old hen by

taking her too soon, and, after her, down with one of the young birds; load quietly and quickly. Daisy stops where she is; up gets another bird and that goes down.

Smoker is sent forward, and he gathers and brings in the old hen and two young birds from out of the deep heather.

No doubt the old cock is a runner.

David and Daisy sit down whilst I go forward and put Smoker on to where the old bird dropped.

We sit and watch him; see the old dog threading the scent at a quick pace in and out amongst the peat hags.

Oh dear, the bird has taken down the burn and we may lose him.

But no; an hundred yards below out comes Smoker from the burn triumphant, with the old cock, which he delivers up without a scratch save the broken pinion.

Daisy is now away to find a fresh point. What has Smoker pointing there, with a look that says as plain as dogs can speak, that fool, Daisy, who thinks so much of herself in her hurry to get fresh points, has left a close sitting bird in that tuft of good heather.

Yes, Smoker is right, as he always is in all he does, and another bird is flushed and bagged.

The brood was seven, and now but two away, thanks to the studious care and intelligence of my two four-footed friends.

And what fine birds, with their white speckled breasts! the young ones as large as the old ones.

Daisy on Point.

We pile them in a heap for the gillie to collect as he comes along.

Dear old Daisy, there were better dogs with better noses and grander action, but the loving creature did her very best to bring birds to bag by care and gentleness, and she did it too.

That retriever, Smoker, the second of his name, has now passed away, and his place taken by a worthy third, was a character.

Amongst other things he was born defective in the power of propagation.

I bred him from a bitch that I bought in Norfolk solely to breed him from; the father was a dog belonging to a keeper of Col. Kenyon Slaney.

There were only two dogs in the litter, all the others being bitches.

He was a poor puny thing, and would have been consigned to the bucket with sundry of his sisters, had there been other dogs in the litter.

But as he grew, and he grew fast, he showed signs of great intelligence.

When old enough, he was sent down to Dalnawillan, to David's care, and there again I saw him when nearly full grown, when there fishing in June.

He knew me again. "Is he steady and quiet, David?"—"Oh, yes." So we took a walk.

He looked at me out of the corner of his eye, as much as to say, "I wonder if he means to be my master: I will have a try"; so he chases a lamb. I came up with him; he drops the lamb, and away again after the same lamb; aye, and once again after that.

The lamb takes to the river, and I after him. I get hold of the lamb and take it ashore, and put it by my side. It was not really hurt, but in a sad state of mind.

At last, up comes Smoker, and receives a real roasting, that satisfies him as to who is to be master, and I trust that retributive justice also satisfied the injured feelings of the lamb.

He was, without exception, the rankest and most determined puppy I ever handled. At times I thought I must give him up; but he repaid my trouble.

At home in the autumn, a pair of partridges were down in some deep feg he was put upon. Up jumped a hare, far more interesting to Smoker, and he away after. Whistle, whistle, yes until you we hoarse; he would not come.

Again the question had arisen as to who was to be master, so I sat myself down a good half-hour before the guilty rascal came to heel; but when he did, and he knew perfectly well what was coming, a hazel stick, cut specially for his education, effectually reminded him.

He lay on the ground, and howled and moaned. Whips were of no effect, he laughed to scorn such mild trifles.

Dogs never mind being thrashed, if they deserve it. Don't do it oftener than you can help, and then do it effectually.

Smoker gets up, wags his tail, has a bit of biscuit to cement renewed friendship, limps a good deal, and goes to work, and cleverly gathers first one and then the other bird.

Only for me would he work. Not a dump did he care for keeper or any other body, but just went his own wilful way.

He was gentle as a lamb. Little children and small dogs might do as they liked with him. My daughter's pug regarded him with a mixture of intense jealousy and reverence, but that did not prevent Toby from occasionally attacking him tooth and nail, much to the amusement of Smoker.

He was free of the library, and a constant partaker of five o'clock tea when not out at work.

For many years Smoker, in the season, worked on grouse, with Daisy, a setter bitch, and with other dogs.

There was great jealousy between him and Daisy, but both good natured over it.

Daisy was very fond, if she could manage to elude attention, of quietly retrieving a bird, and it was as good as a play to observe her delight and his indignation at her encroachment upon his part of the work.

I could tell endless tales of his ability and intelligence.

When not at work, he was the laziest of dogs, but any symptoms of shooting about he was all life. His great object was, then, to get hold of my shooting cape. He had some idiotic notion that he had a lien upon me by so doing, and that I was bound to go out to shoot.

On one occasion I was away from home, and a lady in the house induced him to walk with her in the garden.

As she went through the porch, she took my walking stick.

Smoker, presently, in his quiet, gentlemanly way, took hold of the stick, as the lady thought, to carry it. But no, Smoker walks back and deposits it in the porch, as much as to say, "None of that, when my master is away."

In my time, I have had many good pointers and setters.

I have no prejudice as to which, but pointers are more easy to break ; but, then, in those northern latitudes they do not stand the cold so well as setters do.

In breeding, you may reckon that out of four puppies, you will not get more than two out of the four that turn out fairly well, and for dogs of exceptional intelligence not one in twenty ; ay, in fifty.

Rap, who pointed my first Scotch grouse was, take him all in all, as good a pointer as I ever had.

Grace, a setter bitch that I worked at the same time as Rap, was charming in every way.

She was a puppy of the Rûg breed from North Wales. How I came by her I forget, and from her I bred many good dogs, but never anything of exceptional excellence.

The best setter I ever handled was Ben, an ivory coloured setter, a first cross between a Gordon and a Laverack.

He was perfect in his work, but a bit rank if the whip was spared.

He would go to the dead birds after they were down

if he possibly could, that is, if he had the least licence granted to him.

Pointing and retrieving were all one to him.

He would watch a towered or a stung bird, and let him go and he would go straight, judging distance well, a thing very few retrievers can do; and if the bird did not rise again, he would to a certainty bring him.

The only retriever that I have seen judge distance with a towered bird was a large black dog belonging to the late Sir Stephen Glyn. He marked the bird; the ground being difficult he went, not straight, but across other fields to the right of his bird.

I never did any good with red Irish setters, but it does not follow that, others may not have done so, but I very much doubt it.

I was persuaded to buy a beautiful young pedigree bitch puppy, warranted from dogs that on both sides were worked on grouse. She was perfect in shape and colour, but the veriest fool that ever ranged a moor.

After a season's experience not work, for she never did any work except range beautifully, David said that I had better shoot her.

No, I said; I will advertise her in *The Field*, and I did as follows :—

"A very handsome —— pedigree red Irish setter bitch, useless on the field, no nose; probably make a winner on the show bench."

I had several applications, and got a few pounds for her, which I handed to David.

DISEASE.

Touching on the very vexed question of the cause of disease, I will say very little; as to its effects I have said a great deal.

If the poultry fancier keeps a lot of old birds about him, or too thick upon the ground, disease breaks out amongst them.

I take it that on all moors at the end of six and seven years after the last attack, there will be a lot of old birds, and, as with the poultry, disease breaks out and is contagious, and Nature asserts her rights for the survival of the fittest.

The districts west of Dunkeld are probably the healthiest in all Scotland, and so there birds resist disease, but disease has even there made a clearance, and will again.

Yorkshire grouse are now all driven; the old birds come first and are killed off, and we all know that since driving came into vogue, Yorkshire birds are far more healthy.

Were it permissable to hunt the ground in the northern Scotch counties at end of July, and kill off the old birds of the brood, which could be readily done, it would probably stamp out, or at any rate, postpone, the attacks of disease.

————o-o◦❋◦o-o————

WILDFOWL.

One other matter is worthy of note in Caithness, and that is the steady yearly decrease of wildfowl.

The upper Caithness moors are breeding ground for wildfowl, geese, ducks, widgeon, teal, plover, and snipe, all, or nearly all, make their way down to the lower ground, so soon as they can flap or fly.

They are not killed in the country to any extent, and if reduced by shooting, it must be by the punt guns in the south, weilded by Sir Ralph Payne Galwey and his colleagues.

As to golden plover, where seventeen years back there were a dozen pairs in the spring time, there will not be more than one or two.

A number of arctic birds nest on the flows, gulls of various kinds—the skua gull, redshanks, and green-shanks (a rare bird), black ducks, divers, and many others.

In the late October, there are considerable flocks of snow buntings.

CONCLUSION.

My tale is now told. Despite the many bad seasons, the many disappointments, the rod and the gun have kept me going, more or less, year by year, and will, I trust, again, upon the home manor, the trout loch, and the salmon pool, and I have nothing to regret in my Glenmarkie and Dalnawillan leases.

They have afforded me, occasionally, splendid sport, and endless pleasure to my family and to myself.

The fine air of Caithness, direct from the Arctic Pole, the good water, and the healthy exercise, have contributed to their good health and mine, and to their well being, far more than trips to the English coast, or the Continent, whilst the lads have been made good sportsmen with rod and gun, and their holiday pursuits have given them genuine, honest tastes, as well as healthy recreation.

SUMMARY.

Twenty-four years of Glenmarkie and Dalnawillan leases have resulted in nine splendid seasons; five middling ditto; one very middling; and nine with practically no shooting.

On Dalnawillan and Rumsdale moors, the number of grouse killed by sportsmen were as follows :—

	Dalnawillan. Brace.	Rumsdale. Brace.	Total. Brace.
1872	1098	—	1098
1873	151	—	151
1874	—	—	—
1875	38½	—	38½
1876	112	100	212
1877	426½	300	726½
1878	627½	480	1107½
1879	1338	900	2238
1880	1473	1600	3073
1881	822	900	1·722
1882	186	370	556
1883	53	—	53
1884	300	170½	470½
1885	635½	439	1074½
1886	1211½	673	1884½
1887	1223	561	1784
1888	816½	500½	1317
	10,512	6994	17,506
Yearly average	618½	411½	1030

I

In addition, in the seasons of 1879, '80, '81, '86 and '87, a considerable number of grouse were killed in the winter months by the keeper.

THE END.

SCHULTZE GUNPOWDER.
IMPROVED, WATERPROOFED.—NEW ISSUE.
Manufactured at the Works of the Schultze Gunpowder Company Limited, Eyeworth Lodge, Hampshire.

TRADE   MARK.

THE powder now offered to the public possesses all the good qualities of former issues, viz., greater penetration, closer and more even pattern, less recoil, less report, less smoke, and less fouling than any other explosive; it has no prejudicial effect upon the barrel, and has the additional advantage of being practically unaffected by damp or heat.

It may be used in Small-bore Rifles with good results.

PIGEON SHOOTING.
ALL THE PRINCIPAL EVENTS OF LATE YEARS.

THE GRAND PRIX DU CASINO, MONTE CARLO 1886, 1887, 1888, 1889
THE HURLINGHAM CUP.......................... 1886, 1887, 1888, 1889
THE GUN CLUB INTERNATIONAL CUP 1886, 1887, 1888, 1889
THE MEMBERS' CHALLENGE CUP, 42 times out of 54 competitions.

And during the present season, up to date, prizes FOUR TIMES greater in value than those obtained by all other powders combined have been won by gentlemen using

"SCHULTZE POWDER."

The powder is used by the best Pigeon Shots at home and abroad.

Each Canister bears a Label, with the Trade Mark as above.

To be had Retail and in Cartridges from all respectable Dealers, and by Traders Wholesale at the Offices of

THE SCHULTZE GUNPOWDER COMPANY LIMITED,
32, GRESHAM STREET, LONDON, E.C.

AGENCIES.—United States: 8, Murray-street, New York. Canada: H. S. Howland, Sons, and Co., Toronto. India: Manton and Co., Calcutta; Treacher and Co. Lim., Bombay; Oakes and Co., Madras. Victoria: H. Abrahams and Co., Melbourne. Italy: 23, Piazza Nuova, Genoa. Ireland: Cambridge and Co., Carrickfergus.

CAUTION.—"Schultze" is the oldest, best known, and most reliable Smokeless Powder, and the public is cautioned against inferior and imitation powders.

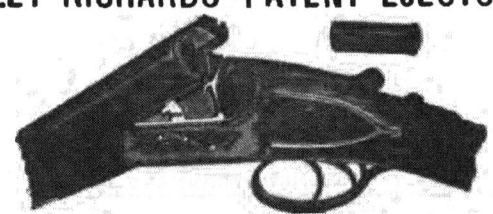

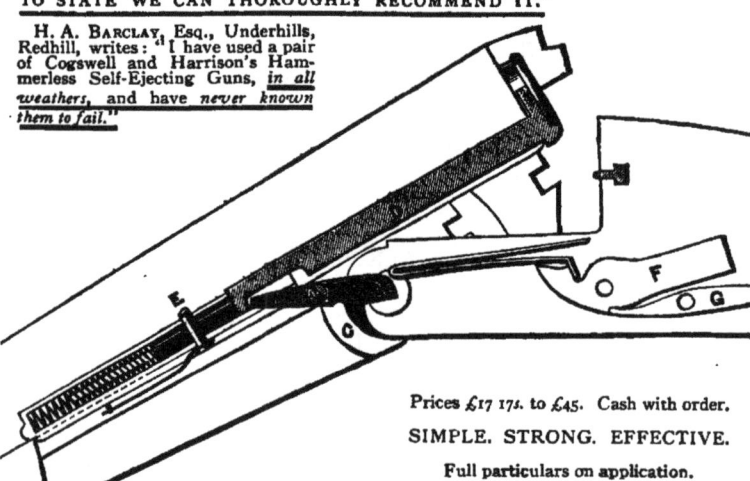

1889

A

CATALOGUE OF BOOKS

RELATING TO

Angling, Boating, Cricket, Farming, Gardening, Hunting,
Shooting, Tennis, Travel, Yachting, &c.,

USEFUL FOR

COUNTRY GENTLEMEN,

TRAVELLERS, ETC..

PUBLISHED BY

HORACE COX,

"THE FIELD" OFFICE, 346, STRAND, LONDON, W.C.

** *Orders for any of the following works, with postage
stamps or post-office order (payable at the Money Order Office,
369, Strand) for the amount, should be sent to* HORACE COX,
*Publisher, at the above address, or they may be obtained by
order of any bookseller.*

NOTE.

I BEG to call the attention of Country Gentlemen, Travellers, Sportsmen, Farmers, and others to the works quoted in this Catalogue. They are written by authors who are well known and acknowledged authorities on their respective subjects.

The illustrations have been intrusted to competent artists, and neither pains nor expense have been spared to make the works as complete as possible.

HORACE COX,

Publisher.

A
CATALOGUE OF BOOKS

PUBLISHED BY

HORACE COX.

Second Edition, Greatly Enlarged.

Royal 4to., bevelled boards, gilt edges, price 15s., by post 15s. 9d.

PHEASANTS:

THEIR

NATURAL HISTORY AND PRACTICAL MANAGEMENT.

BY

W. B. TEGETMEIER, F.Z.S.,

(Member of the British Ornithologists' Union.)

AUTHOR OF "THE NATURAL HISTORY OF THE CRANES," &C.

Illustrated with numerous full-page engravings drawn from Life by T. W. WOOD.

CONTENTS.

The Natural History of the Pheasants, Habits, Food, Structure, &c.; Management in Preserves and in Confinement, with detailed descriptions of the Different Species adapted for the Covert and the Aviary, and an account of their Diseases and Transport.

NOTICES OF THE SECOND EDITION.

From Yarrell's "British Birds," fourth edition.—"For further details, as well as for instructions as to the management of pheasants, both in the covert and the aviary, and the disorders to which they are liable, the reader is referred to Mr. Tegetmeier's excellent work, to which the editor is under great obligations."

From the *Pall Mall Gazette.*—"This new and sumptuous edition contains so large an amount of fresh matter that it may be regarded, practically, as another work. In its own way, it is quite exhaustive. Illustrated by admirable and life-like full-page illustrations. On the technical details of rearing and preservation, Mr. Tegetmeier will be found a thoroughly trustworthy and scientific guide."

From the *Daily Telegraph.*—"Both in its description and practical aspects, the treatise is admirable."

"THE FIELD" OFFICE, 346, STRAND, W.C.

Super-royal 8vo., price £2 2s., by post £2 3s.

YACHT ARCHITECTURE.

By DIXON KEMP,

Associate Institute Naval Architects (Member of the Council).

THIS WORK enters into the whole subject of the laws which govern the resistance of bodies moving in water, and the influence a wave form of body and wave lines have upon such resistance. It also deals comprehensively with the subject of STEAM PROPULSION as applied to yachts. An easy SYSTEM for DESIGNING is provided, and every necessary calculation is explained in detail. The latter part of the work is devoted to YACHT BUILDING, and engravings are given of every detail of construction and fitting, including laying off, taking bevels, &c. The List of Plates (exclusively of over thirty devoted to the elucidation of the text, and nearly two hundred woodcuts) exceeds fifty, and comprises the LINES of some of the most CELEBRATED YACHTS AFLOAT by the most successful builders and designers.

SUMMARY OF CHAPTERS.

Chap.
I.—Displacement, Buoyancy, and Centre of Buoyancy explained.
II.—Proportions of Yachts and Tonnage Rules; Rules for Freeboard, Depth, &c.
III.—Stability as influenced by the Proportions. Form. Weight, and Ballasting of Yachts; their Centres of Gravity and Buoyancy. Profusely Illustrated.
IV.—The Motions of Yachts among Waves as influenced by their Forms and Proportions.
V.—Lateral Resistance, and the adjustment of its centre in relation to the Centre of Effort of the Sails.
VI.—Power to Carry Sail; the Impulse of the Wind as a Propelling Force Apportioning Sail for Speed; Speed Formulæ, &c.
VII.—The Action of the Rudder and Steering Efficiency. Proportions of Rudders, &c.
VIII.—Resistance of Vessels moving in Water. The Wave Line Theory; the Stream Line Theory; the Wave Form Theory. Mr. Froude's Admiralty Experiments, clearly defining the exact influence of Form on Speed.
IX.—Resistance Experiments with Models.
X.—The Wave Form in Theory and Practice. The Forms of many celebrated Yachts analysed.
XI.—Steam Yachting. The Boiler, Engine, Indicator, &c., practically explained at great length.
XII.—Propulsion by Steam. The action of the screw propellor and all the conditions which influence propulsion by steam explained, with numerous practical examples.
XIII.—Rules and Formulæ in use for determining the Displacement, Stability, and other qualities of a yacht fully explained.
XIV.—Working Examples for making all the necessary Calculations concerning a Yacht, every sum being given in detail.
XV.—Yacht Designing: being a complete system for putting into effect the Art of Designing Yachts by Scientific Methods.
XVI.—Laying Off, Making Moulds, Taking Bevels, &c.; Taking Off a Yacht's Lines, &c.
XVII.—Yacht Building: Giving detailed examples for constructing yachts, with numerous plates and engravings of the various parts of the vessel, including two large coloured lithographs on a half inch scale giving sectional views of a 40-tonner, complete with all her fittings, &c.
XVIII.—Spars and Blocks. Rules for fixing upon their lengths, girths, &c. Sizes of block, cordage, &c.
XIX.—Ballasting.
APPENDIX.—Contains much information concerning small yachts, various useful tables, &c.

"THE FIELD" OFFICE, 346, STRAND, W.C.

In two volumes, imperial 8vo., cloth, price Three Guineas.
Originally published at Five Guineas.

THE

FISHES OF GREAT BRITAIN

AND

IRELAND.

By FRANCIS DAY, F.L.S., F.Z.S., &c.

Mr. HORACE COX begs to announce that he has purchased the copyright of this valuable Standard Work, and has very much reduced the price, in order to render it more easily available to Students of Natural History.

THIS WORK CONTAINS NEARLY 200 PLATES AND MANY WOODCUTS.

In one volume, imperial 8vo., cloth, price One Guinea.
Originally published at Two Guineas.

WITH TWELVE COLOURED PLATES AND MANY WOODCUTS.

BRITISH AND IRISH SALMONIDÆ.

By FRANCIS DAY, C.I.E., F.L.S., and F.Z.S.

This work is an exhaustive treatise on the Salmonidæ of the British Islands, and will be interesting to the fisherman, and a text-book to the scientific icthyologist. The reduced price will place it within the reach of all.

ILLUSTRATED WITH FULL-PAGE ENGRAVINGS DRAWN PRINCIPALLY FROM LIFE BY HARRISON WEIR.

In Imperial 4to., bevelled boards, gilt edges, price 18s., by post 18s. 9d.

THE

CATTLE OF GREAT BRITAIN:

BEING

A SERIES OF ARTICLES

ON THE

VARIOUS BREEDS OF CATTLE OF THE UNITED KINGDOM, THEIR HISTORY, MANAGEMENT, &c.

EDITED BY THE LATE JOHN COLEMAN,

Editor of the Farm Department of "The Field," and formerly Professor of Agriculture at the Royal Agricultural College, Cirencester.

ILLUSTRATED WITH FULL-PAGE ENGRAVINGS DRAWN PRINCIPALLY FROM LIFE BY HARRISON WEIR.

In Imperial 4to., bevelled boards, gilt edges, price 18s., by post 18s. 9d.

THE

SHEEP AND PIGS OF GREAT BRITAIN:

BEING

A SERIES OF ARTICLES

ON THE VARIOUS

BREEDS OF SHEEP AND PIGS OF THE UNITED KINGDOM, THEIR HISTORY, MANAGEMENT, &c.

EDITED BY THE LATE JOHN COLEMAN,

Editor of the Farm Department of "The Field," and formerly Professor of Agriculture at the Royal Agricultural College, Cirencester.

"THE FIELD" OFFICE, 346, STRAND, W.C.

NEW AND CHEAPER EDITION OF THE CATTLE, SHEEP, AND PICS OF CREAT BRITAIN.

Now ready, with Illustrations from the Original Drawings by Harrison Weir, in 1 vol., price 12s. 6d., by post 13s.

The Cattle, Sheep, and Pigs of Great Britain:

Being a Series of Articles on the Various Breeds of the United Kingdom, their History, Management, &c.

Edited by the late JOHN COLEMAN,

Editor of the Farm Departmen of "The Field" and formerly Professor of Agriculture at the Roy Agricultural College, Cirencester.

CONTENTS.

THE CATTLE OF CREAT BRITAIN.

I.—Introductory.
II.—Breeding and Genera Management.
III.—Principles of Feeding, and Value of Different Kinds of Food.
IV.—Buildings, and the Management of Manure.
V.—Dairy Management, the Milk Trade, &c.
VI.—Shorthorns. By John Thornton.
VII.—The Hereford Breed of Cattle. By T. Duckham.
VIII.—Devon Breed of Cattle. By Lieut.-Col. J. T. Davy.
IX.—The Longhorns. By Gilbert Murray.
X.—The Sussex Breed of Cattle. By A. Heasman.
XI.—Norfolk and Suffolk Red-Polled Cattle. By Thomas Fulcher.
XII.—Galloway Cattle. By Gilbert Murray.
XIII.—The Angus-Aberdeen Cattle.
XIV.—The Ayrshire Breed of Cattle. By Gilbert Murray.
XV.—West Highland Cattle. By John Robertson.
XVI.—The Glamorgan Breed of Cattle. By Morgan Evans.
XVII.—Pembrokeshire or Castlemartin Cattle. By Morgan Evans.
XVIII.—The Anglesea Cattle. By Morgan Evans.
XIX.—The Kerry Breed of Cattle. By the late R. O. Pringle.
XX.—The Jersey Breed of Cattle. By John M. Hall.
XXI.—The Guernsey Breed of Cattle. By "A Native."

THE SHEEP OF CREAT BRITAIN.

I.—Introductory.
II.—The Management of Ewes up to Lambing.
III.—Preparations for and Attention during Lambing.
IV.—Management from Birth to Weaning.
V.—From Weaning to Market.
VI.—On Wool.
VII.—Leicester Sheep.
VIII.—Border Leicesters. By John Usher.
IX.—Cotswold Sheep.
X.—Long-Woolled Lincoln Sheep.
XI.—The Devon Long-Wools. By Joseph Darby.
XII.—Romney Marsh Sheep.
XIII.—Southdown Sheep.
XIV.—The Hampshire or West Country Down Sheep. By E. P. Squarey.
XV.—Shropshire Sheep.
XVI.—Oxfordshire Down Sheep. By Messrs. A. F. M. Druce and C. Hobbs.
XVII.—The Roscommon Sheep. By the late R. O. Pringle.
XVIII.—Negrette Merino Sheep.
XIX.—Exmoor Sheep.
XX.—The Black-faced or Scotch Mountain Sheep.
XXI.—Cheviot Sheep. By John Usher
XXII.—Dorset Horned Sheep. By Joseph Darby.
XXIII.—Welsh Mountain Sheep. By Morgan Evans.
XXIV.—The Radnor Sheep. By Morgan Evans.
XXV.—Herdwick Sheep. By H. A. Spedding.

THE PICS OF CREAT BRITAIN.

I.—Introductory.
II.—The Berkshire Pig.
III.—Black Suffolk Pigs.
IV.—Large White Breed of Pigs.
V.—Small White Pigs.
VI.—Middle Bred White Pigs.
VII.—The Black Dorset Pig.
VIII.—The Tamworth Pig.

"THE FIELD" OFFICE, 346, STRAND, W.C.

SIXTH EDITION.

Super-royal 8vo., price 25s., by post 26s.

A MANUAL

OF

YACHT AND BOAT SAILING.

BY

DIXON KEMP, A.I.N.A.,

AUTHOR OF "YACHT DESIGNING."

(The Lords Commissioners of the Admiralty have ordered this work to be supplied to the Libraries of the ships of the Royal Navy.)

THIRD EDITION (REVISED 1889). *Price 7s. 6d., by post 7s. 10d.*

A SYSTEM OF FIGURE SKATING.

BY

By H. E. VANDERVELL AND T. MAXWELL WITHAM

(Members of the Skating Club).

The present Revised Edition contains a New Chapter describing the Club Figures, which will enable country skaters to perfect themselves in the art of combined skating.

FOURTH EDITION. *In post 8vo., limp cloth, gilt, price 2s. 6d., by post 2s. 8d.*

THE ART OF SKATING;

WITH

ILLUSTRATIONS, DIAGRAMS, AND PLAIN DIRECTIONS FOR THE ACQUIREMENT OF THE MOST DIFFICULT AND GRACEFUL MOVEMENTS.

By GEORGE ANDERSON ("Cyclos"),

Vice-President of the Crystal Palace Skating Club, and for many years President of the Glasgow Skating Club.

"THE FIELD" OFFICE, 346, STRAND W.C.

PUBLISHED ANNUALLY.

Now ready, Vol. II., 1888–89, price 2s. 6d., by post 2s. 10d.

THE GOLFING ANNUAL

Edited by JOHN BAUCHOPE.

*** The attention of golfers is called to this work, which differs from kindred publications in many respects. It contains Original Articles, not merely Reprints; and its Club Directory is the only Complete and Accurate List of Golf Clubs and Descriptions of Golf Greens ever published.

THIS WORK CONTAINS ABOVE 700 PAGES, AND NEARLY 400 ILLUSTRATIONS.

*New and cheaper Edition, with additions, price 25s., by post 26s.
cloth gilt.*

Shifts and Expedients

OF

CAMP LIFE, TRAVEL, and EXPLORATION.

BY

W. B. LORD AND T. BAINES.

(Royal Artillery.)   *(F.R.G.S.)*

CONTENTS.

"THE FIELD" OFFICE, 346, STRAND, W.C.   c

Demy 8vo., pp. 483, price 15s., by post 16s.

THE

MODERN SPORTSMAN'S GUN AND RIFLE,

INCLUDING

GAME AND WILDFOWL GUNS, SPORTING AND MATCH RIFLES AND REVOLVERS.

Vol. I.—Game and Wildfowl Guns.
Vol. II.—The Rifle and Revolver.

By the late J. H. WALSH,

"STONEHENGE," EDITOR OF "THE FIELD,"

Author of "Dogs of the British Islands," "The Greyhound," "British Rural Sports," &c.

Price 3s. 6d., by post 2s. 9d.

YACHT RACING CALENDAR AND REVIEW.

BY

DIXON KEMP, A.I.N.A,

Author of "Yacht and Boat Sailing," &c.

CONTAINING

ALL THE MATCHES REPORTED IN *THE FIELD* FOR
THE SEASON OF 1888, TOGETHER WITH SUCH OTHER
MATTER AND ILLUSTRATIONS AS MAY BE OF
VALUE FOR REFERENCE TO YACHTSMEN.

"THE FIELD" OFFICE, 346, STRAND, W.C.

Demy 4to., with 12 full-page illustrations, some of which contain Portraits of Sporting Celebrities, and 24 vignettes, price £1 1s., by post £1 2s.

SPORTING SKETCHES

WITH

PEN AND PENCIL.

BY THE LATE

FRANCIS FRANCIS AND A. W. COOPER.

CONTENTS.

Crown 4to., printed on toned paper, price 15s., by post 16s.

THE

ANNALS OF TENNIS.

BY

JULIAN MARSHALL.

THIS work will be found very complete, and, it is thought, justly entitled to take its place as the standard work on Tennis. It has cost its author much laborious research; and, independently of its great value to tennis players and all lovers of the game, it is trusted, from the vast amount of curious lore it contains, the volume will be found not unworthy of a place on the shelves of the scholar. The author, himself a well-known amateur, is fully competent to speak with authority on the game, having had the opportunity of studying the play of the best Continental, in addition to that of the best English, masters, and, therefore, may be taken as a safe guide by learners.

CONTENTS.

"THE FIELD" OFFICE, 346, STRAND, W.C.

A PRESENTATION VOLUME FOR CLUBS.

4to., bevelled boards, gilt edges, (500 pages), with appropriate illustrations, price One Guinea, by post £1 2s. 4d.

THE

ENGLISH GAME OF CRICKET:

COMPRISING A DIGEST OF ITS

ORIGIN, CHARACTER, HISTORY, AND PROGRESS,

TOGETHER WITH

AN EXPOSITION OF ITS LAWS AND LANGUAGE.

BY

CHARLES BOX,

Author of "The Cricketers' Manual," "Reminiscences of Celebrated Players," Essays on the Game, "Songs and Poems," "Theory and Practice of Cricket, &c.

CONTENTS.

Large post 8vo., price 6s. 6d., by post 6s. 10d.

Sketches of Life, Scenery, and Sport in Norway.

BY REV. M. R. BARNARD, B.A.,

Author of "Sport in Norway and Where to Find It," "Life of Thorvaldsen," and Translator of "Private Life of the Old Northmen," &c.

This work is admirably adapted for use as a Sporting Tourist's Handbook, while it is of absorbing interest to the general reader.

"THE FIELD" OFFICE, 346, STRAND, W.C.

Price 1s., by post 1s. 1d.

PASTURES, OLD AND NEW:

A Plea for the Improvement of Old Turf, Better Systems of Grassing-down, and the Prolonged Tenure of Alternate Husbandry Grass Layers.

By JOSEPH DARBY.

SECOND EDITION, *large post 8vo., price 5s., by post 5s. 3d.*

ANGLING.

BY THE LATE

FRANCIS FRANCIS.

Author of "A Book on Angling," "By Lake and River," "Hot-Pot," &c.

CONTENTS.

Post 8vo., in cloth, price 5s., by post 5s. 4d.

HOT-POT.

MISCELLANEOUS PAPERS

BY THE LATE FRANCIS FRANCIS,

Author of "A Book on Angling," "By Lake and River," "Angling," &c

CONTENTS.

A Christmas Reverie—The First Day of the Season—A Strange Fishing Match—The Poacher—The Banker—Reminiscences of an Angler; or, Justices' Justice—Christmas in the Fisherman's Snuggery—St. May Fly—Catching Tartars—Under the Boughs, "Now and Then"—Reminiscences of an Angler, "Farmer Gumshun"—Bankers and Tinkers—The Pleasures of Grayling Fishing—Will Whistle—An Angler's Christmas Yarn—Reminiscences of an Angler, "Squaring the Keeper"—A Week on the Brattle—A Storm on the Brawle—White Trout and Salmon Fishing in Galway—Reminiscences of an Angler, "Anglers' Miseries"—Sam Coventry—Piscatory Prosings "De Omnibus Rebus," &c.—Chewton Pike.

"THE FIELD" OFFICE, 346, STRAND, W.C. *d*

Small post 8vo., price 2s. 6d., by post, 2s. 10d.

THE

ARCHER'S REGISTER

FOR

1888-89.

EDITED BY FRED. T. FOLLETT,

Archery Correspondent to "The Field."

CONTENTS.

PART I.—Reports of Public Meetings in 1888—Percentages—Averages of Scores at the Public Meetings—Comparison of the Total Hits and Scores—Greatest Number of Hits and Scores—Highest Scores and Hits made on each Day, and Total Scores—Highest Scores made at Private Club Meetings—Gentlemen's Scores over 900 (Double York Round)—Ladies' Scores over 700 (Double National Round).   By A. Henty.

PART II.—Review of the Season 1888, by the Rev. C. H. Everett.—Arrow Marks and Arrow Ribbons, by W. K. R. B.—John o' Gaunt's Centenary, by F. T. F. —Archery in Regent's Park Thirty Years Ago—An Archery Medal, by W. K. R. B.—Three Golds' Feat.   Poetry: Flirting Arrows, by Avonvale; The Boy and the Ring, by the Earl of Lytton.   In Memoriam: James Sharpe (with Portrait), late Editor of "The Archer's Register;" William Hammond Solly; Arthur Thomas Malkin; Sir William Frederick Pollock, Bart.

PART III.—Private Clubs Prize Meetings, Scores, Matches, &c.—Aberdeen Archery Club—American National Archery Association—Ohio State Archery Association.

In crown 8vo., with Thirteen full-page Plates, price 2s. 6d., by post 2s. 9d.

THE SWIMMING INSTRUCTOR:

A TREATISE ON THE ARTS OF SWIMMING AND DIVING.

By WILLIAM WILSON.

Author of "Swimming, Diving, and How to Save Life," "The Bather's Manual," "Hints on Swimming."

Demy 8vo., with folding plates and full-page illustrations printed on toned paper, price 21s., by post 21s. 9d.

MODERN WILDFOWLING.

BY

LEWIS CLEMENT,

" WILDFOWLER."

"THE FIELD" OFFICE, 346, STRAND, W.C.

SECOND EDITION. *Large post 8vo., price 7s. 6d., by post 8s.*

THE

"IDSTONE" PAPERS.

A SERIES OF ARTICLES AND DESULTORY OBSERVATIONS ON SPORT AND THINGS IN GENERAL.

BY

"IDSTONE,"

OF "THE FIELD."

CONTENTS.

WORK BY THE LATE FRANCIS FRANCIS.

In crown 8vo., price 3s. 6d., by post 3s. 9d.

ANGLING REMINISCENCES.

By the late FRANCIS FRANCIS,

Author of "A Book on Angling," &c.

CONTENTS.

"THE FIELD" OFFICE, 346, STRAND, W.C.

Large post 8vo., price 3s. 6d., by post 3s. 9d.

PRACTICAL PHEASANT REARING:

WITH AN APPENDIX ON GROUSE DRIVING.

By RICHARD JOHN LLOYD PRICE,

Author of "Rabbits for Profit and Rabbits for Powder," &c.

CONTENTS.

Chap.
I.—The General History of the Pheasant — Treating of the Pheasant and its Egg.
II.—The Barn Door Hens.
III.—The Eggs and the Appliances necessary for Hatching.
IV.—Hatching Out—The Incubator.
V.—The Rearing Field — Protection from Vermin.
VI.—Moving of the Coops and Treatment of the Young Birds.

Chap.
VII.—Recipes for the Preparation of and Instructions for the proper Administration of the Food to Young Pheasants.
VIII.—The Diseases of Young Pheasants and their Cure.
IX.—Catching up, Moving into Coverts, and the proper Food for Older Birds.
X.—Miscellaneous Remarks, and a few Words on Turkeys.

APPENDIX.—HINTS ON GROUSE DRIVING.

Chap.
I.—Practical Hints on Driving Grouse.
II.—Practical Hints on Driving Grouse (continued).

Chap.
III.—The Working of the Drive, and the Duties of the Drivers.

In post 8vo., with Illustrations, price 3s. 6d., by post 3s. 9d.

THE PRACTICAL MANAGEMENT OF FISHERIES.

A BOOK FOR PROPRIETORS AND KEEPERS.

By the late FRANCIS FRANCIS,

Author of "Fish Culture," "A Book on Angling," "Reports on Salmon Ladders," &c. &c. &c.

CONTENTS.

Chap.
I.—Fish and Fish Food.
II.—How to Grow Fish Food and how to Make Fishes' Homes.
III.—On the Management of Weeds and the Economy of Fishing.
IV.—The Enemies of Trout and how to Circumvent them.
V.—The Artificial Incubation of Ova.

Chap.
VI.—On the Rearing of Fry and the Conduct of Ponds, Stews, &c.
VII.—Some Hatcheries.
VIII.—Coarse Fish.
IX.—On Salmon and Trout Ladders and Passes.
APPENDIX.—Notes, &c.

Price 2s. 6d. by post 2s. 9d.

GAME REGISTER,

GIVING AN ACCOUNT OF EACH HEAD OF GAME KILLED, AND HOW DISPOSED OF.

Containing also Divisions for Registering Sporting Engagements and General Observations.

"THE FIELD" OFFICE, 346, STRAND, W.C.

VOLUME I. and II. (containing Parts I. to VI.), in crown 8vo., red cloth, price 6s., by post 6s. 6d.

THE

HUNTING COUNTRIES
OF
ENGLAND,
THEIR FACILITIES, CHARACTER, AND REQUIREMENTS.
A GUIDE TO HUNTING MEN.

By "BROOKSBY."

CONTENTS.

PART I.—Introduction—The Belvoir—The South Wold—The Brocklesby—The Burton and The Blankney—The Fitzwilliam—The Quorn—The Cottesmore—The Puckeridge—The Old Berkeley.

PART II.—The North Warwickshire—The Pytchley—The Woodland Pytchley—The Atherstone—The Billesdon or South Quorn—The Meynell—The Bicester and Warden Hill Hunt—The Heythrop—The Old Berkshire—The South Oxfordshire—The South Nottinghamshire—The East Kent—The Tickham—The Vine—The South Berkshire—Mr Garth's—The H. H.—The Tedworth—Lord Ferrers'—The Warwickshire.

PART III.—The Dulverton—The Stars of the West—Mr. Luttrell's—Lord Portsmouth's—The Essex and the Essex Union—The Hertfordshire—The Whaddon Chase—The Vale of White Horse—The Cheshire and South Cheshire—The Blackmoor Vale—The Cambridgeshire—The Duke of Grafton's—The Holderness—The Oakley—The North Herefordshire—The Duke of Buccleuch's—The Tynedale—Lord Percy's—The Morpeth—The Rufford.

Also now ready (VOLUME II.).

PART IV.—The Badsworth—The Southdown—The East Essex—The Bramham Moor—The East Sussex—The Essex and Suffolk—The York and Ainsty—Lord Fitzwilliam's—The Crawley and Horsham—The West Kent—Sir Watkin Wynn's—The Hursley—The Hambledon—Lord Coventry's—The Grove—The West Norfolk—The Bedale—Lord Zetland's—The Craven—The Surrey Union.

PART V.—The Old Surrey—Mr. Richard Combe's—The Burstow—The Hurworth—The Cattistock—The Suffolk—The Shropshire—The Earl of Radnor—Capt. Hon. F. Johnstone's—The South Durham—The Worcestershire—The Ledbury—The South Herefordshire—The South Staffordshire—The North Staffordshire—The Duke of Beaufort's—The Cotswold—The Dumfriesshire—The Albrighton—The North Cotswold.

PART VI.—Lord Middleton's—The Sinnington—The Wheatland—The United Pack—The Chiddingfold—Lord Fitzhardinge's—Hon. Mark Rolle's—South-and-West Wilts—Lord Portman's—The Cleveland—The North Durham—Braes of Derwent—The Radnorshire and West Hereford—The Monmouthshire.

Each Part is published separately, price 2s. 6d.

SECOND EDITION. *Price 2s. 6d., free by post 2s. 8d.*

PRACTICAL DINNERS:
CONTAINING 108 MENUS AND 584 RECIPES.

By " The G. C.,"
"Author of Round the Table.'

"THE FIELD" OFFICE, 346, STRAND, W.C.

Royal 8vo., price 10s. 6d., by post 11s.

HORSE BREEDING RECOLLECTIONS.

BY

COUNT G. LEHNDORFF,

CONTAINING:

Notes on the Breeding of Thoroughbreds—In-breeding and Out-crossing—Pedigrees of all the Principal Sires—and Genealogical Tables of Celebrated Thoroughbreds.

Post 8vo., price 7s. 6d., by post 8s.

MOSS FROM A ROLLING STONE;

MOORISH WANDERINGS AND RAMBLING REMINISCENCES.

BY

CHARLES A. PAYTON.

" Sarcelle" of " The Field," &c., Author of " The Diamond Diggings of South Africa."

Price 5s. cloth, by post 5s. 4d.

A Year of Liberty; or, Salmon Angling in Ireland.

BY W. PEARD, M.D., LL.B.

SECOND EDITION   *Price 2s. 6d., by post 2s. 8d., in limp cloth.*

RABBITS FOR PROFIT AND RABBITS FOR POWDER.

A Treatise upon the New Industry of

Hutch Rabbit Farming in the Open, and upon Warrens specially intended for Sporting Purposes; with Hints as to their Construction, Cost, and Maintenance.

By R. J. LLOYD-PRICE.

Price 8d., by post 9½d.

THE "FIELD"

LAWN TENNIS UMPIRES' SCORE-SHEET BOOK

[60 SETS],

With Instructions for the Use of Umpires.   Adapted for the Use of Umpires, as used at the Championship Meetings.

"THE FIELD" OFFICE, 346, STRAND, W.C.

8vo., pp. 463, with 32 illustrations, price 16s., by post 16s. 10d.

ESSAYS
ON
SPORT AND NATURAL HISTORY.
By J. E. HARTING.

CONTENTS.
Shooting — Hawking — Fishing — Training Hawks — Lark Mirrors — Plover Catching—Fishing with Cormorants—Decoys—The Irish Wolfhound—The Badger —Wild Turkeys—The Great Bustard—Seals—Wild Swans, &c.
Thirty-eight Essays: concluding with Practical Hints on Bird Preserving for the use of Travellers and Collectors.

In demy 8vo., price 3s. 6d., by post 3s. 9d.

HINTS ON THE MANAGEMENT OF HAWKS.
By J. E. HARTING,
Author of " A Handbook of British Birds," " Essays on Sport and Natural History."

Large post 8vo., price 6s., by post 6s. 4d.

RAMBLES AFTER SPORT;
OR,
TRAVELS AND ADVENTURES IN THE AMERICAS AND AT HOME.
By "OLIVER NORTH."

CONTENTS.
A Week's Duck Shooting at Poole—That Sheldrake—Quail Shooting in California —Bear Hunting in Mexico—Bear Shooting in California—My First Elk—My Last Bear—Round Cape Horn, Valparaiso, Santiago—Andacollo, Lima, Panama, Jamaica—Country Sports and Life in Chile—Shooting in Chile—Two Days' Fishing in Chile—"Toling" for Docks in California—Up the Sacramento—The White Elk of Astoria—Sport in the Coast Range Mountains.

In large post 8vo., limp cloth, price 2s. 6d., by post 2s. 8d.

COLORADO:
ITS
AGRICULTURE, STOCKFEEDING, SCENERY, AND SHOOTING.
By S. NUGENT TOWNSHEND, J.P.
("ST. KAMES.")

"THE FIELD" OFFICE, 346, STRAND, W.C.

*Demy 8vo., printed on plate paper, with Illustrations on toned paper,
price 2s., by post 2s. 4½d.*

A HISTORY AND DESCRIPTION, WITH REMINISCENCES,

OF THE

FOX TERRIER.

BY RAWDON B. LEE,

Kennel Editor of "The Field."

THE ILLUSTRATIONS BY ARTHUR WARDLE.

CONTENTS.

CHAPTER I.—Introductory—Old Writers on Terriers—The Fox Terrier, 1806—Value of Terriers a Century ago—Their Varieties.
CHAPTER II.—Increasing Popularity—Early Shows : Old Jock, Tartar, Old Trap, and Grove Nettle—Disuse of the Fox Terrier with Hounds.
CHAPTER III.—More Notabilities—Ear Dropping and other Malpractices—Forming a Kennel—The Fox Terrier Club—Some Modern Kennels.
CHAPTER IV.—The Fox Terrier Club's Scale of Points—General Opinions—With Otter Hounds—Working and Training Terriers—Coursing Rabbits.
CHAPTER V.—The Wire-haired Fox Terriers—Yorkshire and Devonshire Strains—The Rev. John Russell's Terriers—Crosses—The Best Dogs.
CHAPTER VI.—Breeding and Rearing Puppies—Superfœtation—Preparing for the Show—Trimming—Conclusion.
ADDENDA.—Rules and Officers of the Fox Terrier Club—List of Minor Clubs.

ILLUSTRATIONS.

Jock, Grove Nettle, and Tartar—"Wait Until I've Done" (Vignette)—The Fox Terrier, 1806—Old English Terriers (Vignette)—"A Race for Life" (Vignette)—Portrait of "Result"—Portrait of "Vesuvienne"—"On the Bench" (Vignette)—"What Comes Next" (Vignette)—Portrait of "Carlisle Tack"—Portrait of "Carlisle Tyro"—"Rather Doubtful" (Vignette)—"A Guard at Euston Station" (Vignette"—"A Long, Lean, Evenly-marked Head" (Vignette).

In handy pocket size, price 1s. 6d., by post 1s. 7d.

THE GAMEKEEPER'S SHOOTING MEMORANDUM BOOK

FOR THE

REGISTERING OF GAME SHOT, MEMORANDA OF SALE, &c.

By I. E. B. C.,

Editor of "Facts and Useful Hints relating to Fishing and Shooting," "The Game-keeper's and Game Preserver's Account Book and Diary," &c.

Crown 8vo., price 2s. 6d., by post 2s. 9d.

PUBLIC SHOOTING QUARTERS

IN ENGLAND, WALES, SCOTLAND, IRELAND, AND ON THE CONTINENT.

By "WILDFOWLER,"

Author of "Shooting and Fishing Trips," "Modern Wildfowling," "Table of Loads," &c.

"THE FIELD" OFFICE, 346, STRAND, W.C.

Demy 8vo., price 5s. 6d., by post 5s. 10d.

THE

ROTHAMSTED EXPERIMENTS

ON THE

GROWTH OF WHEAT, BARLEY, AND THE MIXED HERBAGE
OF GRASS LAND.

BY WILLIAM FREAM.

(B.Sc. Lond., F.L.S., F.G.S., F.S.S.)

SECOND EDITION. *In demy 8vo., price 10s. 6d., by post 11s.*

ESTATE MANAGEMENT:

A PRACTICAL HANDBOOK FOR LANDLORDS, AGENTS,
AND PUPILS,

By CHARLES E. CURTIS.

WITH A

LEGAL SUPPLEMENT BY A BARRISTER,

Extract from Preface.—"He who intends to qualify himself for such interesting and responsible work as the care and oversight of landed property must in these days of keen competition, give up the idea that he need only abandon himself to the pleasures of a country life, and that all needful information will be picked up by the way."

CONTENTS:

Chap.
I.—Letting and Leases.
II.—Farm Valuations.
III.—Forestry.
IV.—Underwood.
V.—Fences.
VI.—Grasses suitable for Woods and Plantations.
VII.—The Home Farm.

Chap.
VIII.} Repairs and Materials.
IX.}
X.—The Blights of Wheat and other Cereals.
XI.—Accounts.
XII.—Useful Rules of Arithmetic and Mensuration.

In crown 8vo., price 1s., by post 1s. 1d.

CATECHISM OF ESTATE MANAGEMENT.

SECTION I.

LETTING AND LEASES.

By CHAS. E. CURTIS, F.S.I.,

Professor of Estate Management at the College of Agriculture, Principal of the School of Estate Management, Author of "Estate Management," &c.

"THE FIELD" OFFICE, 346, STRAND, W.C.

SECOND EDITION, Greatly Enlarged (with Illustrations and Plans of Silos).

Price 6s., by post 6s. 6d.

SILOS
FOR
PRESERVING BRITISH FODDER CROPS STORED IN A GREEN STATE.

Notes on the Ensilage of Grasses, Clovers, Vetches, &c.

COMPILED AND ANNOTATED
BY THE

EDITOR OF "THE FIELD."

CONTENTS.

Price 6d., by post 7d.

SHORT NOTES ON SILO EXPERIMENTS AND PRACTICE.

(Extracted from "Silos for Preserving British Fodder Crops.")

"THE FIELD" OFFICE, 346, STRAND W.C.

Price 6d., by post 7d.

HARVESTING CROPS INDEPENDENTLY OF WEATHER:

Practical Notes on the Neilson System of Harvesting.

By "AGRICOLA,"

AND OTHER CONTRIBUTORS TO " THE FIELD."

In crown 8vo., price 2s. 6d., by post 2s. 8d.

MANURES:

THEIR RESPECTIVE MERITS FROM AN ECONOMICAL POINT OF VIEW.

BY A. W. CREWS

Author of " Guano : its Origin, History, and Virtues," " The Potato and its Cultivation," &c.

CONTENTS.

PART. I.—Definition of the Word "Manure"—Nature's Modes of Applying Fertilisers—History—Classification.

PART II.—The Value of Ploughing Down Green Crops—Weeds—Sea-weed—Straw—Sawdust—Tanners' Bark—Wood Ashes—Peat—Rape Cake—Hemp-Poppy, Cotton, and Cocoa-nut Cakes—Bran—Malt Dust—Brewers' Grains—Coal—Soot—Charcoal.

PART III.—Dead Animals—Fish—Blood—Animalised Charcoal—Bones—Horn—Woollen Rags, Hairs, Feathers, &c.—Night-soil—Farmyard Manure—Guano.

PART IV.—Salts of Ammonia—Salts of Magnesia—Salts of Potash—Salts of Soda—Common Salt—Lime and its Compounds—"Ooze."

In crown 8vo., price 2s., by post 2s. 2d.

THE POTATO AND ITS CULTIVATION.

BY A. W. CREWS.

Author of " Guano : its Origin, History, and Virtues," " Manures : their Respective Merits, &c.

CONTENTS.

Derivation — History — Constituents — Varieties — Sprouting — Soils — Planting—Manures—Earthing up—Disease—Scab—Storing—Forcing—Producing New Varieties—Substitutes for the "Potato"—Miscellaneous Information.

" THE FIELD " OFFICE, 346, STRAND, W.C.

FIFTH EDITION.

*Re-written, with additions and new full-page Engravings. In one
volume, bevelled boards, gilt edges, price 15s., by post 15s. 9d.*

THE

DOGS OF THE BRITISH ISLANDS:

BEING

A SERIES OF ARTICLES

ON

THE POINTS OF THEIR VARIOUS BREEDS,

AND

THE TREATMENT OF THE DISEASES TO WHICH THEY ARE SUBJECT.

REPRINTED FROM " THE FIELD" NEWSPAPER.

BY THE LATE

J. H. WALSH,

"STONEHENGE," EDITOR OF "THE FIELD."

(WITH THE AID OF SEVERAL EXPERIENCED BREEDERS.)

Demy 8vo., price 3s. 6d., by post 3s. 9d., Illustrated with several Diagrams.

THE

PRACTICAL SURVEYOR:

A TREATISE UPON SURVEYING.

SPECIALLY ARRANGED FOR THE GUIDANCE OF PUPILS, STEWARDS,
THE SCHOLASTIC PROFESSION, AND INTENDING EMIGRANTS.

BY THOMAS HOLLOWAY.

Price 6d., by post 7d.; or 2s. 6d. the half-dozen.

"THE FIELD" DUPLICATE JUDGING BOOK

Facilitates the work of the Judges at Poultry and other Shows, by a very simple
method of entering and preserving a duplicate judging list.

"THE FIELD" OFFICE, 346, STRAND, W.C.

SECOND EDITION. *In Three Parts, large post 8vo., price 5s., by post 5s. 4d., each.*

THE

FARM, GARDEN, AND STABLE.

By I. E. B. C.,

Editor of " The Gamekeeper's and Game Preserver's Account Book and Diary."

CONTENTS.

Part I.—The Farm.
Cattle—Crops—Dairy—Diseases—Fencing—Food for Stock—Manures—
Miscellaneous—Pigs—Sheep—Soils—Weeds—Woods.

Part II.—The Garden.
Flowers—Fruit—Houses—Lawns—Manures—Miscellaneous—Seeds—Trees and
Shrubs—Vegetables—Vermin—Weeds.

Part III.—The Stable.
Carriages—Diseases—Feeding—Harness, &c.—Miscellaneous—Stable Management.

PUBLISHED ANNUALLY. *In large post 8vo.*

THE

KENNEL CLUB STUD BOOK:

CONTAINING A COMPLETE

RECORD OF DOG SHOWS AND FIELD TRIALS,

WITH

Pedigrees of Sporting and Non-Sporting Dogs.

Vol. I., from 1859 to 1873, price 12s. 6d., by post 13s.

PRICE 10s. 6d., BY POST 10s. 10d. EACH—

Vol. III., 1875; Vol. IV., 1876; Vol. V., 1877; Vol. VI., 1878;
Vol. VII., 1879; Vol. VIII., 1880; Vol. IX., 1881; Vol. XI., 1883;
Vol. XII., 1884; Vol. XIII., 1885; Vol. XIV., 1886; Vol. XV., 1887.

Demy 8vo., price 1s., by post, 1s. 1d.

THE EARLY MATURITY OF LIVE STOCK

By HENRY EVERSHED,

Writer on Agriculture in the "Journal of the Royal Agricultural Society of
England," "The Field," "Quarterly Review," &c.

"THE FIELD" OFFICE, 346, STRAND, W.C.

PUBLISHED ANNUALLY. *Demy 4to., price 1s., by post 1s. 2d.*

THE RURAL ALMANAC

AND SPORTSMAN'S ILLUSTRATED CALENDAR FOR 1889.

Articles on the following Subjects are included in the List of Contents:

THE PAST RACING SEASON.
LIST OF HUNTS, THEIR MASTERS, &c.
FIELD TRIALS WITH POINTERS AND SETTERS.
CANINE MATTERS, WITH COMPLETE LIST OF CLUBS.
A FIGHT WITH A SALMON.
SILVER-BODIED AND OTHER FLIES, WITH RECIPES FOR
    PRESERVING SALMON FLIES.
ARTIFICIAL TROUT POND.
IMPROVEMENT OF POOR WET PASTURES.
HIGHEST PRICED SALES OF THE YEAR.
RAW v. COOKED FOOD FOR CATTLE.
SUCCESSIVE CROPS OF CORN.
THE BIGGEST BAG OF GROUSE.
MUSHROOMS ALL THE WINTER.
GLASSHOUSE GARDENER.
POULTRY KEEPING FOR CHICKENS AND EGGS.
AUSTRALIAN CRICKETERS IN 1888.
THE COUNTY CRICKET SEASON.   TENNIS IN 1888.
INTERNATIONAL SPEED SKATING.
STALLIONS FOR BREEDING BLOODSTOCK AND HUNTERS
    (List of about 300 Stallions, with their Pedigrees, and Fees for
    Thoroughbred and Half-Bred Mares).

ALSO SUMMARIES, TABLES, RECIPES, &c., VIZ.,

Angling close seasons
Artificial fox earth
Athletic championships
Beagles, packs of
Bicycling, best times on record
Boat-races, Oxford and Cambridge
Boots, waterproof dubbing for
Brown leather boots, cleaning
Cambridgeshire winners
Cesarewitch winners
Close seasons for game
Derby winners
Dog clubs, list of
Dogs for India
Eggs, preserving
Fairs for horses, &c.
Foxhounds, packs of
Game, legal season for killing
Grease in horses' feet, cure of
Harriers, packs of

Horses kicking, cure for
Huntsmen, changes of
Jumping records
Lawn, improving the turf of
Oaks winners
Otter hounds, packs of
Public Schools athletics in 1888
Races of 1889, dates of
Racquets, Schools challenge cup
Running, best times
St. Leger winners
Swimming, amateur performances
Tennis, University matches
Terms, University and Legal
Tricycling performances
University athletic sports
University boat-races
University racquet matches
University tennis matches
Walking, best times.

"THE FIELD" OFFICE, 346, STRAND, W.C.

In crown 8vo., price 5s., by post 5s. 4d.

BOAT-RACING;

OR,

THE ARTS OF ROWING AND TRAINING.

BY

EDWIN DAMPIER BRICKWOOD

(EX-AMATEUR CHAMPION OF THE THAMES).

CONTENTS.

PUBLISHED ANNUALLY.   *Price 1s., by post 1s. 1d.*

THE ROWING ALMANACK AND OARSMAN'S COMPANION FOR 1889.

Edited by E. D. BRICKWOOD

(EX-AMATEUR CHAMPION OF THE THAMES),

Author of "Boat-Racing; or, the Arts of Rowing and Training."

CONTENTS.

"THE FIELD" OFFICE, 346, STRAND, W.C.

FOURTH EDITION. *In demy 4to., on toned paper, and in fancy cover, price 2s.,*
by post 2s. 2d.

THE BOOK OF DINNER SERVIETTES ;
CONTAINING

A NEW INTRODUCTION ON THE DECORATION OF DINNER TABLES,
AND GENERAL DIRECTIONS FOR FOLDING THE SERVIETTES.

There are Twenty-one different kinds given, with Ninety-two Woodcuts Illustrative
of the various Folds required, and the Serviettes complete.

Price 5s., by post 5s. 2d.

"COMBINED FIGURE SKATING;"

Being a collection of 300 combined figures, as skated by the Skating Club, London,
the Wimbledon Skating Club, &c., illustrated by 130 scaled diagrams, showing the
correct direction of every curve executed by the skater, and the recognised amount
of circling round the centre; together with a progressive series of alternate
"calls." The figures are named in accordance with the revised system of nomen-
clature and rules for combined figure skating, compiled by the Skating Club,
London, Sept. 11, 1882. Diagrams of the combined figures in the first and second
class tests of the National Skating Association are included.

BY MONTAGU S. F. MONIER-WILLIAMS AND STANLEY F. MONIER-WILLIAMS
(Members of the Wimbledon Skating Club).

Post free, 6d., cloth gilt.

RULES OF THE GAME OF HOCKEY
AND OF
THE HOCKEY ASSOCIATION.

Price 1s., by post 1s. 1d.

NOTES ON THE PROOF OF GUNS.
TOGETHER WITH
THE NEW RULES AND SCALES OF PROOF PASSED BY THE
SECRETARY FOR WAR, AND COMMENTS THEREON.

Price 1s., by post 1s. 1d.

TATTERSALL'S RULES ON BETTING,
WITH EXPLANATORY NOTES AND COMMENTS,

Containing an Account of Cases decided by Tattersall's Committee, with a Copious
Index, and the Rules of Racing appended.

By G. HERBERT STUTFIELD, Barrister-at-Law,
Author of the "Law Relating to Betting, Time Bargains, and Gaming."

"THE FIELD" OFFICE, 346, STRAND, W.C.

REPORTS on SALMON LADDERS, with Original
Drawings, Plans, and Sections. By FRANCIS FRANCIS. In post 4to., price
2s. 6d., by post 2s. 7d.

A MANUAL of the LAW of SALMON FISHERIES in
ENGLAND and WALES, with a copious Index. By SPENCER WALPOLE.
one of Her Majesty's Inspectors of Salmon Fisheries. Price 2s. 6d., by post 2s. 8d.

A TABLE of CALCULATIONS for use with the "Field"
Force Gauge for Testing Shot Guns. Also an Illustration and Description
of the Apparatus. In demy 4to., price 2s. 6d.

THE RULES of PIGEON SHOOTING. Published by
Special Permission, the Hurlingham Club and the Gun Club Rules of Pigeon
Shooting. SECOND EDITION. Bound together in cloth, gilt edges, price 6d., by
post 7d.

THE COURSING CALENDAR, for the Spring Season
1889, contains Returns of all the Public Courses run in Great Britain and
Ireland. A revised List of Addresses of Coursing Secretaries. Public Coursers,
Judges, Slippers, and Trainers, with List of Waterloo Cup Winners, Greyhound
Sales, &c. Edited by C. M. BROWNE ("ROBIN HOOD"). Price 10s. 6d.

Price 6d., by post 6½d.
OFFICIAL EDITION OF THE LAWS OF LAWN TENNIS.
THE LAWS of LAWN TENNIS for the year 1889,
issued under the authority of the LAWN TENNIS ASSOCIATION.

Price 6d., by post 7d.
OFFICIAL EDITION OF THE REGULATIONS FOR THE MANAGEMENT
OF LAWN TENNIS PRIZE MEETINGS.
REGULATIONS for the MANAGEMENT of LAWN
TENNIS PRIZE MEETINGS and INTER-COUNTY and INTER-CLUB
MEETINGS, issued under the authority of the LAWN TENNIS ASSOCIATION.

Price 1s. 6d., by post 1s. 9d.
THE "FIELD" LAWN TENNIS CALENDAR for
1889. Containing a List of Secretaries and their Addresses; the Laws of
Lawn Tennis; Regulations for the Management of Lawn Tennis Prize Meetings
and Inter-County and Inter-Club Meetings; Report of the Meeting of Representatives; and a Full Report o all the Meetings of the last Season, &c.

THE ITALIAN SYSTEM of BEE KEEPING; being an
Exposition of Don Giotto Ulivi's Economical Frame Hives and Honey
Extractor. By Arthur J. Danyell, late Capt. H.M. 31st Regiment. With Illustrations. Price 1s., by post 1s. 1d. This pamphlet contains practical, directions for
the making and utilisation of frame hives, costing less than 2s. each, and a centri-
fugal honey extractor costing 5s. or 6s.

In 4to., printed on toned paper, with plates, price 5s., by post 5s. 4d.

THE QUEEN LACE BOOK:

AN

Historical and Descriptive Account of the Hand-made Antique Laces of all Countries.

BY L. W.

This work contains the whole of the series of articles on Antique Point Lace which have been published in "The Queen." It will prove an invaluable guide, and book of reference to ladies interested in Antique Lace, and, with its highly ornamental embossed cover, will form a handsome ornament for the drawing-room table.

ENGLISH TRANSLATIONS OF THE CLASSICS.

Post 8vo., 540 pages, price 7s. 6d.

HALF-HOURS WITH GREEK AND LATIN AUTHORS.

FROM VARIOUS ENGLISH TRANSLATIONS, WITH BIOGRAPHICAL NOTICES.

By G. H. JENNINGS and W. S. JOHNSTONE,

Authors of a "A Book of Parliamentary Anecdote."

In post 8vo., price 5s., by post 5s. 4d.

THE BARB AND THE BRIDLE:

A

HANDBOOK OF EQUITATION FOR LADIES,

AND

MANUAL OF INSTRUCTION IN THE SCIENCE OF RIDING FROM THE PREPARATORY SUPPLING EXERCISES ON FOOT TO THE FORM IN WHICH A LADY SHOULD RIDE TO HOUNDS.

By "VIEILLE MOUSTACHE."

Handsomely bound in cloth, price 3s. 6d., by post 3s. 9d.

ACTING CHARADES FOR OLD AND YOUNG.

BY

ARTHUR LILLIE

Author of "The Enchanted Toasting Fork," &c.

In paper cover, price 6d.

"THE QUEEN" RECIPES.

By "THE G. C." (Author of "Round the Table").

"THE QUEEN" OFFICE, 346, STRAND, W.C.

Price One Shilling ; by Post, 1s. 3d.

THE QUEEN ALMANAC,

AND

LADY'S CALENDAR for 1889.

AMONG ITS CONTENTS WILL BE FOUND

A CHROMO-LITHOGRAPH PLATE OF DESIGNS

FOR EMBROIDERY IN COLOURS, ETC.

TWO COLOURED PLATES OF NOVELTIES IN KNITTING
AND CROCHET.

Specimens of China Painting ; Instructions in Cameo Cutting ; Speci-
mens of Art Carving, &c. ; Art Pottery and Glass, Repoussé Work,
Hammered Iron, &c. ; Suggestions for Table Decorations, Fancy
Needlework, &c. ; Artistic Arrangement of Rooms ; Evening
Toilettes, Headdresses, Jewellery, &c.

TWENTY-FIVE PORTRAITS:

Among others, Portraits of the Princess of Wales, late Emperor
Frederick III. and Empress Dowager of Germany, the present Emperor
and Empress of Germany. the King and Queen of Sweden, Prince and
Princess Oscar of Sweden, &c.

ALSO

Fashionable Mantles, Dresses, and Headdresses for Indoor and Out-
door wear; Winter Mantles and Hats ; Children's Costumes, Hats,
and Toques; Suggestions for Fancy Costumes; Lingerie, Under Linen,
and Children's Costumes ; Suggestions for Ornamental and Useful
Arrangements of Flowers and Plants ; Chip Carving, &c.

Full information is given relating to—The Royal Family ; the Royal Household ;
the Government ; British and Foreign Ambassadors ; Lord Lieutenants of Counties
in the United Kingdom ; Irish and Scotch Representative Peers ; Peers who are
M'nors ; Peeresses in their own right ; Alphabetical List of the Surnames of the
Peers Temporal ; Complete List of the House of Peers, with their Surnames and
Titles, and the Titles of their Eldest Sons ; Jewish Calendar ; Bank of England ;
Post Office Regulations ; Eclipses in 1889 ; List of Charities, Associations, &c.
Obituary of Ladies of Distinction during the Past Year.

RECIPES FOR SOUPS, BREAKFAST DISHES, AND HORS D'ŒUVRES.

"THE QUEEN" OFFICE, 346, STRAND, W.C.